BRITAIN IN OLD PHOTOGRAPHS

BRISTOL 1920–1969

DAVID J. EVELEIGH

Budding BOOKS

First published in 1998 by
Sutton Publishing Limited · Phoenix Mill
Thrupp · Stroud · Gloucestershire · GL5 2BU

This edition first published in 2001 by
Budding Books, an imprint of
Sutton Publishing Limited

Title page: A woman with her daughter receiving attention from a housing office, *c*. 1948, *see* p. 119.

British Library Cataloguing in Publication Data
A catalogue record for this book is available from the British Library.

ISBN 1 84015 192 7

Typeset in 10/12 Perpetua.
Typesetting and origination by
Sutton Publishing Limited.
Printed in Great Britain by
J.H. Haynes & Co., Sparkford.

The towers of All Saints' church (left) and Christ church rise above Fry's factories in this mid-1930s city centre roof-t view.

CONTENTS

	Introduction	5
1.	The Port & Docks	9
2.	Trade & Industry	27
3.	The City Centre	47
4.	Retailing & Victualling	73
5.	Housing & Domestic Life	95
6.	Leisure & Recreation	123
7.	Local Government & Services	135
8.	Bristol Blitzed	149
	Acknowledgements	159
	Bibliography	160

Park Street from the Art Gallery, *c.* 1950. One of the principal shopping streets in the city, Park Street was badly damaged during the blitz and at the time of this view there were still several large gaps in the street. They were later filled, however, with façades matching the original buildings. The bus advertising George's beers is on its way to Henbury and is painted in the new post-war green livery. In the distance the CWS building and the Royal Hotel stand out against the city centre haze, while the presence of the City Docks is marked by several cranes.

INTRODUCTION

Another book of old photographs of Bristol? My initial response was surely there will be little demand, when the idea of a title in Sutton Publishing's Britain in Old Photographs series was first suggested. Over forty volumes of Reece Winstone's books, plus a large number of other works, has resulted in a strong photographic record of Bristol in print. Nevertheless, the book went ahead. The original idea was to cover the hundred years from 1850 to 1950 but it soon became clear that there was sufficient material for two books, and so the first was published two years ago under the title *Bristol 1850–1919*. The book concentrated on Bristol's expansion and modernisation in Victorian and Edwardian times, concluding with a section on the city's contribution to the First World War.

This second volume continues the record from 1920, beyond 1950, to 1969. This fifty-year period effectively covers the mid-twentieth century, and while many previous books on Bristol have split this into three separate periods (the inter-war years of the 1920s and 1930s, the Second World War from 1939 to 1945 and the post-war era, particularly concentrating on the city in the 1950s), I have chosen to group these together in order to emphasise continuity in the city's development between the 1920s and 1960s. However, the book is not organised chronologically and does not attempt a 'blow-by-blow' account of the city in this period. Instead, the photographs are arranged thematically into eight sections looking at the port, trade and industry, the city centre, retailing, home life, leisure, local government and services and the Second World War. The impact of the war (throughout the text 'the war' refers exclusively to the Second World War, 1939–45) is evident in virtually every aspect of life in the city but the photographs in the final section convey something of the awfulness of life in war-time Bristol.

Enemy bombing wrought terrible damage to the centre of Bristol and the inner suburbs – parts of Bedminster, for example, suffered badly; but this was only one of several major factors affecting the development of mid-twentieth century Bristol. Greater involvement of government – central and local – in town planning and the provision of services and amenities played a major part in shaping the city in this period. In particular, the City Council tightened its hold on the overall development of Bristol:

regional plans made jointly with Bath and other neighbouring urban districts were first drawn up in 1925 and continued to be produced through the 1930s – but they were only advisory; it was the 1947 Town & Country Planning Act which transformed the City Council's role from one of mere regulation to active control of the city's development. Henceforward, the city planners' vision for Bristol was backed by law and so the city's first Development Plan published in 1952 had a major bearing on the city's development until the late 1960s – not only because of the breadth of its scope, but because it defined the city's chief priorities: the building of new homes and the control of traffic.

The provision of housing by the Council – which became mandatory after 1919 – was an area where the local authority made a conspicuous contribution to the development of the city in this period and one which radically altered the lives of thousands of people. By the 1960s roughly 40 per cent of Bristol's population lived in council houses which set new standards of accommodation. The mid-twentieth century saw a general rise in the standard of living with particularly marked rises in the 1930s and 1950s; it was in the 1930s that home ownership first became a major national trend and in Bristol (as elsewhere) this was represented by the building of many thousands of private houses. The 1930s also saw electricity supplies reach most homes and the acquisition of the first electric domestic appliances, while the 1950s and 1960s saw a revolution in levels of expectation for most people, with an even wider level of ownership of domestic and personal consumer goods, including electric washing machines, television sets and motor cars. The levels of comfort and convenience in the home – and the time available for leisure – were a world apart from the Bristol of 1920.

Motorised traffic has played a major part in shaping the development of the city since the end of the First World War. In 1920, apart from taxis and trams owned by the Bristol Tramways & Carriage Company – and thousands of bicycles – most of the traffic on the roads was horse drawn. Car ownership was a luxury restricted to the wealthy. But the 1920s saw a rapid increase in private motor cars while horse-drawn carts and wagons began to give way to motorised vans and lorries. The consequences were enormous: new words entered everyday language – motorists, car parks and petrol stations – while the numbers of wheelwrights, farriers and saddlers dwindled to be replaced by motor garages and car mechanics. Most important of all was the increase in the volume of traffic on the streets. There were several issues here, of which safety was one: the early 1930s saw the introduction of traffic lights and belisha beacons to better control junctions and make road crossings safer for pedestrians; motorists began to demand car parks; and, most critically, the extra traffic caused congestion. From the 1930s city planners became increasingly preoccupied with easing and regulating traffic flow through the city, and from then until the 1960s many drastic changes were wrought to the fabric of the city in the name of the motor car.

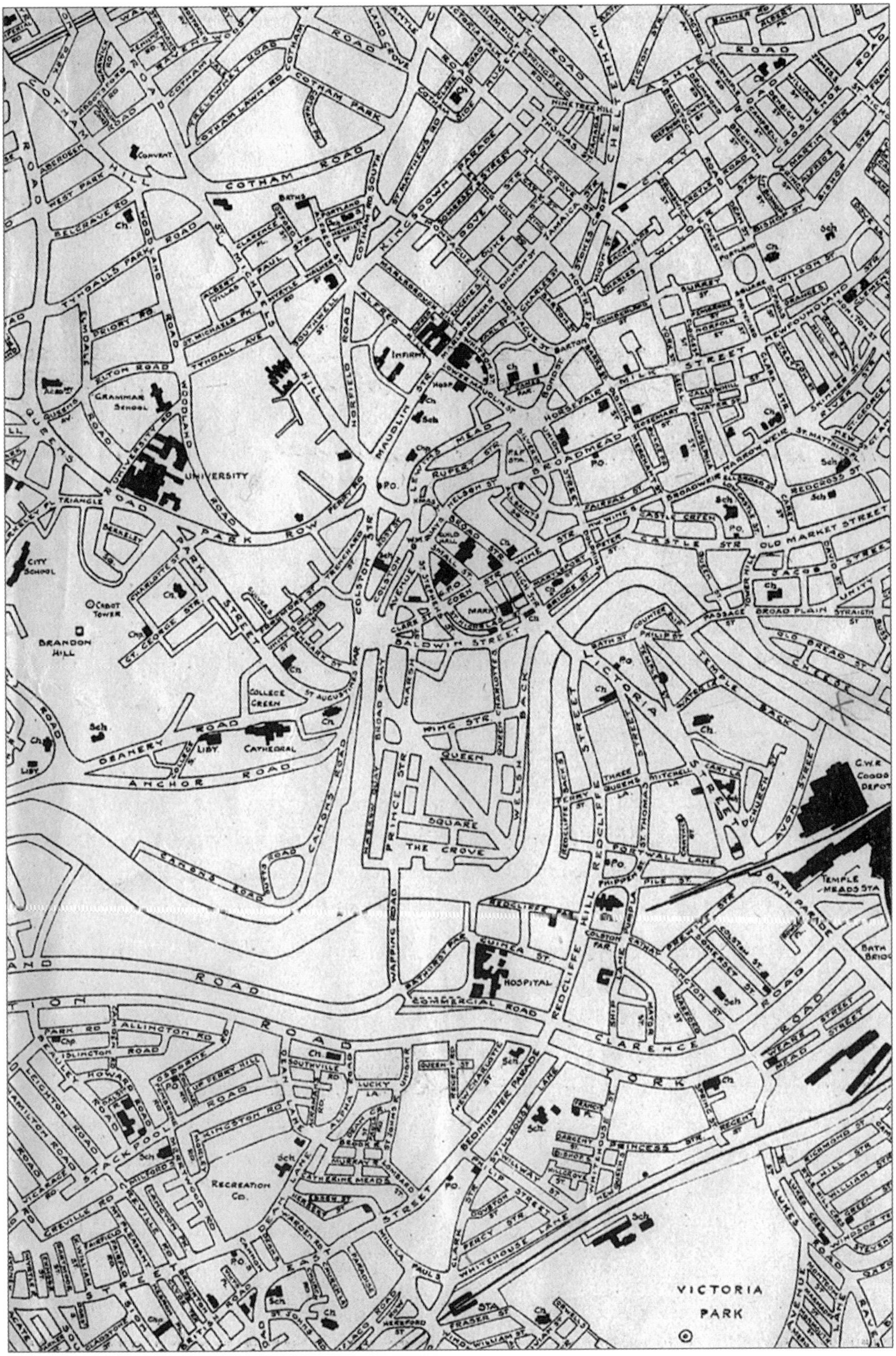

The centre of Bristol, *c.* 1935.

The car and motor bus gave people unprecedented freedom and this was a factor in the expansion of the city. Bristol continued to push out its boundaries into the surrounding countryside: north-westwards to include much of Henbury and the Severnside industrial district and southwards to Withywood, Hengrove and Stockwood. The total acreage of the city increased from 18,436 acres in 1920 to 27,068 acres by 1969. The population also increased, although not as dramatically as the period 1850–1919. In 1920 the population of Bristol was 376,975, reaching a peak of 445,000 in 1955. Thereafter it started to drop, as old housing in the inner city was cleared and because people moved beyond the city boundaries to new urban areas such as Nailsea and Yate. Mid-twentieth-century Bristol, therefore, while a third larger than its Victorian and Edwardian predecessor, was less densely populated.

Searching for the photographs has been an enjoyable, though at times frustrating, exercise: while some subjects are well represented in the photographic record – there is no shortage of photographs of the city centre, for example – other subjects proved elusive and so photographs alone cannot represent every facet of life in the city. The objective, nevertheless, was to make a selection which shows something of the diversity of life in the city, to catch the mood and atmosphere of mid-twentieth-century Bristol and to emphasise the pace of change in this period. For architectural variety, compare the striking modernistic Odeon and showrooms of 1938 (see p. 64) with the timber-framed house in King Street (see p. 92); for contrasts in living conditions over time, compare the scullery of the house in Old Quarry Road – typical of the 1920s – (see p. 111) with the modern all-electric laundry in the council block in 1960. For mood, the group of photographs taken on a council estate in about 1947 convey the optimism of post-war reconstruction, the 'brave new world' that was being forged out of austerity (see pp. 116–117). The photographs also show some well-known buildings such as the Dutch House, a victim of the blitz in 1940 (see p. 57), and the Shot Tower on Redcliff Hill (see p. 31), a victim of a 1960s road-widening scheme; these remind us of the many changes which have taken place in the city between 1920 and 1969.

CHAPTER ONE

THE PORT & DOCKS

Ships and Bristol, as everyone knows, are inseparable. Bristol's early development was based on sea-borne trade, and over the centuries the port has exerted a huge influence over the city's economy, its physical character and identity. Until this century much of the city's industrial and commercial life has revolved around the port: major industries such as soap making, leather working, tobacco and chocolate manufacture relied upon raw materials brought in by sea, while many other trades and industries – boat and ship building, sail making, rope making and coopering, for example – developed as an adjunct to the port. The city's arms depict a ship and Bristol Castle, reflecting the strong physical presence of the port in the heart of the city. When the Floating Harbour was created in 1809 by damming up the course of the Avon, some 86 acres of deep water were formed between the western entrance at the Cumberland Basin and Temple Meads to the east, while an arm of the docks – St Augustine's Reach – penetrated the city centre. Here was the 'street of ships' in a unique city landscape where cranes and warehouses rubbed shoulders with fashionable shops, offices and old parish churches. Throughout this period working ships remained an everyday sight in the City Docks – as the photographs show – but they were, nevertheless, in slow decline and the number of ships using the Floating Harbour fell rapidly in the late 1960s and early 1970s.

By the 1920s Bristol's position as one of the country's leading ports was based on the docks at Avonmouth and Portishead. These had been built in the 1870s by separate companies – in competition with each other and the Corporation-owned City Docks – to attract the larger ships of the second half of the nineteenth century, which were unable to negotiate the tortuous journey up the Avon to the city or even be accommodated in the Floating Harbour. In 1884 they were taken over by the City Corporation and in 1926 a new committee, the Port of Bristol Authority, was created to run all three dock sites. Although Avonmouth had been absorbed within the city boundaries in 1904, the docks 'down the mouth' at Avonmouth and Portishead existed as exclusive dock environments. They were out of sight save for those who worked in them, and never captured the imagination of Bristolians and visitors as did the old City Docks.

Avonmouth Docks had been greatly enlarged in 1908 by the opening of the Royal Edward Dock, connected to the original dock of 1877 by a junction cut, and it was here rather than at Portishead that much of the subsequent expansion of the port occurred. The opening of this dock capable of taking any ship then afloat enabled the port to develop trade from beyond its traditional links with Africa and across the Atlantic to new partners particularly in the Far East. In 1921 the Royal Edward Dock was enlarged by a western extension, followed by an eastern arm extension opened in 1928 and further extended between 1939 and 1945. A conspicuous feature of the Royal Edward Dock was the huge dry dock, 875 ft long, where ships could be brought in for repairs and maintenance. This graving dock remained a useful facility throughout the mid-twentieth century, and in 1969 was still the largest in the Bristol Channel.

The volume of trade handled by the port steadily increased between 1920 and 1969 rising from an annual net tonnage of about 2½ million tons in 1920 to just under 8 million tons by 1969. Imported goods far outweighed the value and tonnage of exports: in 1934 exports were 41,463 tons compared to imports of 2,335,460 tons, and although exports – notably of motor cars – increased after the war, rising to roughly 200,000 tons by 1969, they still represented a small percentage of the total goods handled by the port. Throughout this period general cargoes formed an important part of the port's trade, but it was the importation of several important bulk cargoes which dominated in terms of tonnage, value and also in terms of their impact on the dock landscape. Grain and timber were two of these: the former a relatively new trade dating to the second half of the nineteenth century when cheap North American wheat flooded the market, while the import of timber was an old-established trade dating to the late middle ages. Up to 1939 some of the shipments of these two cargoes still arrived on large sailing vessels. By the 1920s grain was one of the port's principal imports and continued to rise in this period: by 1969 roughly one million tons of grain were being shipped into the port – about an eighth of the net tonnage of imports. Grains imported included wheat from North America, maize from North and South America and the Black Sea, and barley from North Africa, Canada and the Black Sea. Granaries and mills were prominent features of the docks in the City Docks and at Avonmouth where the number of granaries increased from two in the early 1920s to five by 1965. After the war grain storage and milling was increasingly concentrated at Avonmouth, and the port's 1954 guide claimed that Avonmouth was the most important centre for milling in the south-west. Timber was unloaded at all three docks, where large stacks of timber piled in extensive yards were prominent features. Softwood for the building trade continued to be shipped in huge quantities from the Baltic and North America, while tropical hardwoods were brought from Africa and the Far East. By 1969, however, the trade in timber was showing signs of decline.

In contrast, the importation of petroleum was a relatively new trade and one that grew steadily throughout this period. In 1902 imports of petroleum were a mere 75,793 tons, but by 1934 had exceeded 600,000 tons and by 1969 had risen to 3,000,000 tons. Oil tankers were berthed in the Oil Basin at the Royal Edward Dock where an extensive system of pipelines connected with the storage tanks, which increased considerably in numbers between 1920 and 1969. Large quantities of zinc concentrates (which contain sulphur) unloaded at Avonmouth went straight to the National Smelting Co.'s works established after the First World War alongside the Royal Edward Dock, where they were processed into zinc and sulphuric acid. Similarly, Bristol's important paper-making, packaging and printing industry was supplied with wood pulp, paper and newsprint.

Imports of food and drink were also important and sustained some well-known and long-established Bristol industries such as tobacco, which continued to provide major business for the port. In the 1920s annual imports of tobacco stood at 20,000 tons – about 25 per cent of the UK total – and by 1969 had risen to 32,000 tons. Between 1905 and 1919 three bonded tobacco warehouses were built by the Corporation at Cumberland Basin, and in the mid-1920s further bonded warehouses of startling white concrete were built overlooking the Floating Harbour at Canon's Marsh and at Winterstoke Road, Ashton, by the Imperial Tobacco Group. The increase in imports of cocoa – supplying the industry at Bournville as well as in Bristol – was dramatic, from 15,881 tons in 1934 to a record total of 49,182 tons in 1969. In the nineteenth century Bristol merchants trading with West Africa – such as the Lucas Brothers (see *Bristol 1850–1919*, page 41) – maintained their own fleets of ships; by the 1930s, however, the port's service with West Africa was in the hands of the Elder Dempster Line. Tea imports also rose, particularly after the Second World War, and by 1969 over half the tea drunk in Britain was passing through the port. Wine and sherry imports again date to the early history of the port. In the 1930s Bristol remained the chief English port for the importation of wine; added to the traditional links with Portugal and Spain, the port had successfully built up business with wine from the Empire.

In the 1930s steamers of the Isthmian Line unloaded canned fruit and fish from San Francisco and other Pacific ports, while vessels of the Federal, Shaw, New Zealand Shipping Co., Commonwealth and Dominion Lines, Shaw and Clan Line imported meat and dairy produce from New Zealand and Australia. The 1928 extension at the Royal Edward Dock included a cold store for the storage of meat and dairy produce to cater for the expanding trade with New Zealand and Australia. Another important trade in the period covered here was the banana trade, which had only begun in 1901 when the first shipment of bananas from Jamaica was unloaded at Avonmouth. In 1912 the part-American-owned Elders & Fyffes line took over the trade, and for over fifty years their distinctive white steam ships with buff funnels – which also carried mail and passengers between Avonmouth and the West Indies – were a familiar sight at Avonmouth. In the 1930s a third of all bananas brought into England were handled at Avonmouth, and it was a heavy blow to the port when Elders & Fyffes transferred the trade to Southampton in 1967.

The passenger service with the West Indies operated by Elders & Fyffes was only one of several ocean passenger services which operated from the port in the 1920s and 1930s. There were sailings to Rangoon on ships of the Henderson and Bibby Lines and to Australia and New Zealand by Bethell, Gwyn & Co.'s lines. The Royal Edward Dock had a passenger station and special trains connected with arriving and departing liners and mainline railway services. There were also services to other British and European ports, although the volume of passenger traffic fell sharply after the war.

Throughout this period the handling of a wide variety of miscellaneous commodities – the port called them general cargoes – remained important, and in 1969 accounted for over one million tons of imports. For their swift dispatch transit sheds were introduced toward the end of the nineteenth century on the quaysides at Avonmouth and in the City Docks. At Canon's Marsh and Dean's Marsh in the city some of the transit sheds were fitted with 2-ton electric cranes mounted on the roof which were capable of unloading cargoes directly from ship's holds. Other sheds were served by tall electric cranes on the quayside, such as those installed in 1951 in front of L & M sheds on Princes Wharf, built on the site of the corporation granary which had been bombed in 1941. Four of these cranes built by Stothert & Pitt of Bath are now preserved *in situ* on their 15 ft gauge track outside L and M sheds now occupied by the Bristol Industrial Museum; together, the sheds, cranes, railway track and other items of quayside furniture preserve a section of the distinctive dock environment within view of the city centre.

Other mechanical handling equipment such as electrically powered hoists, trolleys and trucks was introduced after the First World War, but the movement of many cargoes in the docks still relied heavily on human muscle. The unloading of Jamaican bananas, for example, in spite of the aid of elevators, still required the labour of some 300 men. Thus a large workforce of dockers and stevedores found employment in the docks: in the 1920s there were about 3,000 dockers employed in Bristol. Dockers were general labourers, while stevedores were employed loading and unloading ships. The work was hard, repetitive and dangerous: accidents were common and employment was uncertain. The arrival of a banana boat was regarded as a 'plum' job guaranteeing three days' work, but at other times this large, casual workforce would stand idle waiting for work. In 1922 the Transport & General Workers' Union was founded under the leadership of Ernest Bevin (1881–1951), a Bristol carter who had become a full-time official of the Dock, Wharf, Riverside and General Workers' Union in 1911. The Union sought to decasualise the work, a conflict which remained unresolved until 1967

Canon's Road, 1920s. Originally entitled 'Winter's Golden Ray', this photograph shows motor lorries, horse-drawn traffic and a lone cyclist on the granite sets in Canon's Road. The back of W transit shed on Dean's Marsh is on the left with U and V sheds further back; the City Lead Works of Rowe Brothers & Co. is on the right. They started business in about 1884 as manufacturers of plumbers' goods, but by the inter-war period were selling a wide range of domestic hardware from their showrooms in Victoria Street.

when dockers found security under the 'Jobs for Life' labour agreement. The increase in containerised cargoes, however, in the 1960s allowed for greater mechanical handling, and the sight of quaysides teeming with dockers manhandling goods between ships and road and rail vehicles became increasingly rare.

Railways were another important part of the dock environment. The port served an extensive hinterland reaching as far as the Midlands, the entire south-west, as well as South Wales. Goods to and from the docks were moved via the Severn navigation to the Midlands and by coastal shipping to other ports in England and South Wales, but the railways formed the chief means of bulk long-distance transport for much of this period. The first rail connection with the docks was made in 1872 when the Great Western and Bristol & Exeter railways jointly opened a Bristol Harbour line from Temple Meads through Redcliff to Princes Wharf. In 1906 a new connection to the docks was opened, which left the Portishead line at Ashton Gate and then crossed the New Cut on the bottom of a new, hydraulically operated, double-deck swing bridge. The line then split, one route running beside the New Cut to connect with the existing track at Princes Wharf, while the second crossed the Cumberland Basin by another swing bridge and then continued alongside Hotwells Road, past the gas works, to a new goods depot at Canon's Marsh.

Both the docks at Avonmouth and Portishead had rail connections from the start. The Portishead line actually predated the opening of the docks, having opened in 1867, while the Midland Railway joined forces with the Great Western to create a new route to Avonmouth in time for the opening of the dock in 1877. In the early 1900s the Great Western Railway made further connections between Avonmouth and its main line to South Wales at Patchway and with its route to the Midlands at Filton. The Port Authority's 1935 Guide claimed that all ship's berths, transit sheds, warehouses, granaries and cold stores were served by its own railway lines, which connected with those of the Great Western and London Midland & Scottish Railway. However, competition from road transport gradually increased during this period. In 1926, with the opening of the four-lane Portway, the docks at Avonmouth acquired a direct road link with Bristol and further afield, and this encouraged a switch to the movement of goods to and from the port by motor lorry. From the 1960s the shift to road haulage, especially upon the opening of the M4 and M5 motorways in stages from the mid-1960s, caused a major decline – as elsewhere – in the use of the railways, and by 1969 the quayside railways at Portishead and Avonmouth were little used. In the City Docks much of the network closed in 1964 and 1965, leaving just the section between Ashton Junction and Wapping Wharf. This continued in use for coal traffic until 1986 and now survives as the preserved Bristol Harbour Railway, which operates two Bristol-built dock shunting locomotives formerly owned by the Port Authority.

The closure of the railway lines around the City Docks was, of course, just one part of their decline which had accelerated after the war. In 1946 Charles Hill & Sons' Bristol City Line transferred from the city to Avonmouth Docks, to enable it to operate larger ships and remain competitive on the trans-Atlantic route. By 1951, 90 per cent of the port's trade went through Avonmouth yet the City Docks remained busy, receiving general cargoes coastwise and from the continent. But in the 1960s coastal shipping declined sharply in the face of competition from motorway-borne road haulage and continental traffic, such as the importation of wood pulp, was transferred to the rivermouth docks. It was clear that the City Docks were no longer commercially viable, and in 1969 the City Council applied for an Act to close the City Docks to sea-going traffic; this was obtained the following year. From the late 1960s the number of working ships entering the Floating Harbour declined rapidly. The timber trade finally left the old docks in 1973 and Charles Hill launched their last ship – the *Miranda Guinness* – in 1976. For another thirteen years sand dredgers and the Wessex Water sludge ship – the *Glen Avon* – kept alive the memory of working ships in the City Docks, but they had gone by 1990. Meanwhile, in an age of much reduced global seaborne trade, the port continued to modernise and adapt to new trends, and the 1960s saw the planning of a new dock at the mouth of the Avon – the West Dock – soon to become better known as the Royal Portbury Dock, which opened in 1978.

Junction Lock Bridge, Cumberland Basin, *c.* 1935. Contrasting forms of road transport cross Junction Lock, wh provides access from the Cumberland Basin to the Floating Harbour. The lock was designed by Thomas Howard, t Docks Engineer, and built in 1871. The present bridge was built in 1925 by William Cowlin & Son, Bristol's leadi construction company, with the steel construction by John Lysaght & Sons of the Netham Iron Works, Bristol. Cowli were also responsible for the three massive red brick bonded warehouses which dominate the western end of the doc These were built by the City Corporation to store imported tobacco in secure bonded warehouses, where the tobac was kept under the care of Customs & Excise authorities until required for use. The duty was paid when the tobacco v released for manufacture. The earliest, A Bond, visible behind the bus, was built in 1905 and incorporates a combin steel and cast-iron frame encased in brickwork. B Bond, to the right, was built two years later, and while externally ve similar is structurally quite different, being built by the Coignet system of reinforced concrete. The Nova Scotia Ho beyond the bridge dates to about 1811, and the name may relate to the former maritime trade between Bristol and Nc Scotia. The Cumberland Basin contained a landing stage for livestock shipped from Ireland, which was just beyond t railings on the right, and from here the cattle were taken across the road to the lairs and slaughter houses behind the w on the extreme left; these remained in use until the 1950s and now the area is occupied by housing built in about 1980.

Horse-drawn traffic was still a common sight on roads in the 1930s, although in sharp decline. Approaching the came is a lightweight commercial wagon drawn by a pony. The double-decker bus was to become a familiar part of the stre scene in Bristol (as in other towns and cities) during the rest of the century, but at the time this photograph was taken v still a relatively novel sight. Apart from a short-lived experiment with double-decker buses in 1908–9, the Bris Tramways & Carriage Company relied on single-deck buses until the introduction of the G-type model in 1931. T particular example entered service in 1932 and is seen in the dark blue and white livery of the BT & CC, which last until the Second World War.

Bridge swing at Junction Lock, 11 August 1961. The Ashton swing bridge was last opened in 1934, but the frequent opening of the Junction Lock bridge caused traffic congestion on this principal route to the south-west. Here, holiday traffic is held up by a bridge swing as the *Manja Dan*, a Danish vessel of the Lauritzen line, leaves the docks on her way to Bordeaux. The ship had arrived from Kotka, Finland, two days earlier with a cargo of paper, wood pulp, newsprint, plywood and blockboard. These vessels, with their bright red hulls and cream upper decks, were a familiar site in the City Docks at this time.

View across the Cumberland Basin to Hotwells and Clifton, 1930s. A boy with a cart made from a Sunlight soap box looks over to houses in Hotwells, demolished in 1963 when the elevated roads leading to the Plimsoll Bridge were built. The boy is standing beside the original lock connecting the Cumberland Basin with the Floating Harbour which passed close to the Nova Scotia public house, behind the photographer. The lock was replaced by the present Junction Lock in about 1871 and blocked off.

Cumberland Basin and the New Cut, *c.* 1963. All three tobacco bonded warehouses are seen in this aerial view of the wester approach to the City Docks: C Bond on the left and A and B Bond in the centre of the view. The Cumberland Basin, th entrance to the Floating Harbour, is to the right, while the New Cut, which carries the tidal waters of the Avon south of th docks is in the centre of the view: happily, this photograph was taken at high tide, as at low water the muddy banks of the cu and river beyond present a less attractive picture! The chimney visible centre right marks the location of the Underfall Yard the headquarters and workshops of the Docks Engineer's department. The chimney is part of the hydraulic pumping statio built in 1888 to provide power to operate the swing bridges and lock gates of the Cumberland Basin.

The photograph records the western end of the Docks shortly before the scene was dramatically transformed by th building of the Cumberland road system, designed to ease traffic congestion on the busy route to the south-west. Previousl all traffic leaving the city had to cross the Cumberland Basin by the Junction Lock Bridge before crossing the upper deck o the Ashton Swing Bridge. Traffic congestion was particularly bad when the Junction Lock Bridge was swung to allow ships t travel between the Cumberland Basin, top right, and the main part of the Floating Harbour. Preparations for construction o the new road network, designed by the City Engineer's Department, are evident in this view: buildings have been cleared i Hotwells to make way for the new approach roads to the Plimsoll Bridge which crosses the Cumberland Basin and the New Cut; the foundations of the Fixed crossing at the mouth of the New Cut appear to be in place; and a crane can be seen to th left of B Bond, the westernmost of the three tobacco warehouses.

The Plimsoll Bridge was opened in April 1965 and the upper deck of the Ashton Swing Bridge and the embankment leading to it were removed. In spite of the many slip roads and flyovers designed to keep traffic moving, the Cumberlan Basin road system remains a traffic black-spot, and motorists from the Portishead direction negotiating the difficult crossin towards Ashton must wonder if this particular link was overlooked by the designers! Junction Lock Bridge remains in use t connect Hotwells Road with Cumberland Road, and the lower deck of the Ashton Swing Bridge which carried the railwa line from Ashton Junction to Canon's Marsh and Wapping Wharf was retained and remains in limited use today by stear trains operated by the Bristol Harbour Railway. The railway line to Canon's Marsh was closed in 1965, and the bridg carrying the single track line across the eastern end of the Junction Lock was removed.

View from Brandon Hill of the Canon's Marsh gasworks, *c.* 1950. The gasworks at Canon's Marsh was established in 1823, originally manufacturing gas from whale and seal oil and subsequently coal gas; it ceased production in the 1950s. On the other side of the docks lines of railway trucks can be seen on Wapping Wharf, while beyond lie the densely packed streets of Southville and Bedminster.

City Docks, 26 July 1958. Five large ships are visible in this view. Berthed at Canon's Marsh alongside Y and Z sheds is the *Kamma Dan* of the Lauritzen line, which has probably unloaded a shipment of wood pulp. On the right the Norwegian vessel the *Stalheim* is being towed towards the Cumberland basin by the tug, *John King*, now preserved at the Bristol Industrial Museum; carrying general cargo, the *Stalheim* was on her way to Oslo via Newport. Behind the transit sheds the tobacco bonds built in the 1920s and demolished in 1989 are visible.

St Augustine's Reach, 30 April 1958. Scenes of docking and cargo handling continued to be visible from the city centre into the 1960s, although the quaysides were out of bounds to the general public. Here, timber is being unloaded from the *Crane* on to lorries using one of the roof cranes fitted to U and V sheds. The *Crane* had arrived the previous day from Bordeaux and Tornnay-Charente, carrying wine and brandy and other miscellaneous goods. The vessel left the following day for Dublin before returning to Bordeaux.

Narrow Quay, 11 August 1961. Old warehouses fronting the quay were soon to come down to make way for a new hotel and multi-storey car park. The Co-operative and Wholesale building of 1906 beyond the warehouses survived for another decade before being demolished to make way for Broad Quay House. The granite sets of the quayside survive, however.

St Augustine's Reach, August 1947. Scandinavian wood pulp is being unloaded into road vehicles and lighters from the Swedish ship, the *Inger*, at U shed using the roof-mounted cranes. The lighters – or barges – will carry the pulp up river to the St Anne's Board Mills; they remained an essential part of the City Docks until the 1960s. The *Inger* arrived in the City Docks from Sweden on 24 August 1947, and after 1,500 tons of wood pulp had been unloaded it sailed for Preston on 30 August.

The Bristol Harbour railway, looking towards Temple Meads from the roof of St Mary Redcliffe, *c.* 1950. Opened in 1872, this was the first railway connection with the City Docks, starting from Temple Meads on a brick viaduct before entering a tunnel beneath the churchyard of St Mary Redcliffe and then crossing the Bathurst Basin on a steam-operated bascule (lifting) bridge. Redcliff goods yard, seen here, once handled a large amount of flour and coal traffic but closed in 1962, and closure of the line followed in January 1964.

Advertisement for Coast Lines Limited, 1935. In the mid-1930s Coast Line steamers maintained three services a week from Liverpool and weekly from London, Manchester, Penzance, Aberdeen and other ports. They continued to trade from the City Docks until the 1960s.

Aerial view of Avonmouth Docks, *c.* 1965. By 1920 the greater part of the Port of Bristol's trade was concentrated at Avonmouth; its importance was reflected in the extensions built by the Port Authority in the 1920s and the extensive industrial development which occurred beside the docks. The photograph shows the original dock of 1877 on the right and, in the centre, the junction cut which connected to the much larger Royal Edward Dock of 1908, which was enlarged by the western and eastern arm extensions opened in 1921 and 1928 respectively.

Royal Edward Dock, Avonmouth, 30 June 1954. A general view of the dock showing *Birmingham City* of the Bristol City line at R Berth on the left, *Kent* at O Berth in the centre of the view and in the distance *Florence Holt*, moored alongside a cluster of cranes at T Berth, which is to the right of the main entrance to the docks and immediately to the right of the entrance to the graving dock.

The Blue Funnel liner *Calchas* at S Berth, Royal Edward Dock, Avonmouth, 28 April 1954. Development of trade with the Far East was an important aspect of the port's twentieth-century expansion. The *Calchas* had just arrived from the Far East loaded with timber and a general cargo including pineapples; she left two days later for Swansea. In 1969 Blue Funnel were still advertising fast monthly sailings from the Far East to Avonmouth.

Cuban sugar being discharged from the *Chamois* directly to road and rail vehicles at Avonmouth, 17 June 1953. The railway wagons belong to the Port Authority. The *Chamois* had arrived from Havana on 14 June and left for Quebec on 25 June.

A 1960s view of the west side of the Eastern Arm extension of the Royal Edward Dock, built in 1928 and modernised in the late 1950s and 1960s with new cranes and other bulk-handling equipment. The railway system was also revised to provide a more flexible system, enabling movement of trains of wagons to suit several vessels at different stages of loading or discharging. In this view timber is being unloaded on to flat railway trucks and lorries.

Dockers at Avonmouth Docks handling sacks, 1930s. Goods such as rice, bran, sugar and animal feed arrived at the p in hessian sacks and were unloaded by a casual workforce of dockers and stevedores. Hard toil and uncertain employm were the lot of dockers for most of this period; they were tough, hard men possessed of great physical strength. T adoption of containerisation of loads and the increased use of mechanical handling in the 1960s reduced the demand fc large labour force at the very time that dockers won security of employment.

CHAPTER TWO

TRADE & INDUSTRY

In 1933 J.B. Priestley found Bristol a lively, bustling city, 'earning its living and spending its own money . . . achieving a new prosperity by selling us Gold Flake and Fry's chocolate and soap and clothes and a hundred other things'. The range of Bristol industries was indeed quite remarkable and rooted in the city's early medieval origins, when the woollen industry, soap manufacture, ship building and a wide range of wood, leather and metal trades were sustained by maritime trade. Raw materials, essential for many of the city's industries, were brought in by sea: tallow, leather hides, metals and metal ores, cocoa beans, tobacco leaf and wines and sherry. The variety of industrial activity in the city was further stimulated by Bristol's pre-eminence in the south-west: Bristol traditionally dominated trade over much of the region, and as one of the largest cities in the country (seventh largest in 1940) it contained a large urban market stimulating a demand for almost everything.

In 1940 the Bristol Development Board claimed that there were 2,248 factories and workshops in Bristol representing some 300 different industries. A few of these dominated the city, the manufacture of tobacco products, for example, and chocolate, which made the name Bristol famous world wide. In 1928 the City Council's publication *Bristol Commercially Considered* stated that there were 11,000 people employed in the food, drink and tobacco industries; the paper and printing trades employed nearly as many, accounting for 9,000 jobs in the city; while engineering and allied trades provided 13,592 jobs. The larger factories belonging to companies such as W.D. & H.O. Wills formed major city landmarks. The Wills factories on East Street and Raleigh Road in Bedminster towered over the neighbouring streets of terraced houses. Until they relocated to Keynsham, Fry's factories, eight of them in total, dominated a cramped site around the Pithay, and their factory chimneys were as conspicuous a city-centre landmark as the nearby church towers. There were several other large works in or close to the centre: breweries, flour mills on Redcliffe Back, an electricity generating station (belonging to the Bristol Tramway & Carriage Company) and Llewellin & James's brass foundry on Castle Green. East of the centre at Broad Plain was the impressive factory of Christopher Thomas & Brothers, soap and candle makers, modelled on a Florentine palace, and next to it the Midland Iron Works of Gardiner Sons & Co.; they specialised in the manufacture of architectural iron and brasswork which adorned many important shops, offices and public buildings in the city.

Many other major industries were located in the eastern districts of the city. Beyond Temple Meads barges carried raw materials up river to Barton Hill and St Philip's Marsh, lying either side of the Feeder Canal, where chemical works, glue and paint factories, potteries, gas works and railway engine sheds filled the air with smoke. Barges carried wood pulp transferred from foreign vessels in the City Docks to the large board mills at St Anne's, established in 1912 by Imperial Tobacco, where it was converted into cardboard packaging for tobacco, chocolates, cereals and other foodstuffs. At Crew's Hole there were more chemical works, while south of the Avon at Brislington the Bristol Tramways and Carriage Company had their works for bus construction. The spread of industry continued eastwards beyond the city's boundaries into Kingswood and Hanham in Gloucestershire, where clothing, footwear and brushmaking were carried on: the Kleen-e-ze Brush Company started the manufacture of brushes in Hanham in the 1920s. In the early twentieth century Fishponds became established as a new engineering centre of Bristol.

While the larger firms dominated the local economy there were also many smaller workshop-based industries and trades employing skilled labour: typically these were small family concerns chiefly making household and personal consumer goods. Some had quite a rural flavour and perpetuated traditional handcrafts, for example basket makers or saddlers, such as Shattock & Hunter in Frogmore Street. Until 1953 S. Sale & Sons continued to make clogs in West Street: these were worn by workers at George's brewery, Fry's and other local factories. The making of shoes and leather trunks were two other important leather trades; there were also hatters, tailors and dressmakers and wood and furniture trades including upholstery. Many small businesses were found in or close to the city centre: thus furniture makers and upholsterers were concentrated in St Pauls.

As it didn't rely too heavily on one particular industry, Bristol's economy proved resilient in difficult times such as the early 1920s, when trade was disrupted following the end of the First World War. Bristol also escaped the worst effects of the depression of the early 1930s, although the city did suffer hardship: unemployment reached 10 per cent in these years, and in February 1932 a march by 10,000 demonstrators protesting against unemployment flared into violence in Old Market, and thirty people were injured. The 1920s saw the demise of several formerly important industries. The last glass cones in the city – at Powell and Ricketts bottle works in Avon Street – were fired for the final time in 1923, and in 1925 the Great Western Cotton Works, which had been a major source of employment in Barton Hill since 1838, closed. Coal mining had been in steady decline in the city since the late nineteenth century and the last collieries in the city closed around this time; with them went the brickworks which had used the clay found with the coal seams. The clothing trades contracted from the 1920s, while the footwear industry – one of the largest employers in the early twentieth century – suffered a major decline between 1920 and 1969. Other old-established industries, however, continued to thrive, and there were many firms, such as Fry's, Harvey's and Wills, which had been in business in the city since the eighteenth century. Lead shot continued to be made using the tower on Redcliff Hill that William Watts, the inventor of the process, had built in about 1782. Ferris & Co., manufacturers of pharmaceutical products in Union Street, had been established in 1754, and E.A. & W. Greenslade, brush and plane manufacturers, in 1727.

By the 1920s several new industries were emerging which were to become vital to the city's prosperity in the mid-twentieth century. Most spectacular was the expansion of the aircraft industry following the creation of the British and Colonial Aeroplane Company at Filton by Sir George White in 1910. In 1920 the company changed its name to the Bristol Aeroplane Company, and alongside the manufacture of aeroplanes began the production of aero-engines. After a period of retrenchment up to 1934 production increased in response to the government's rearmament programme, which placed a strong emphasis on air power, and by 1939 the company was the largest single employer in the city, providing jobs to over 18,000 people. During the war the company manufactured the Blenheim, the Beaufighter and other military aircraft and also produced 101,000 engines. After the war the company developed the Bristol Brabazon as a long-haul passenger aircraft. The prototype made its maiden flight in 1949 among much local optimism: at the time this handsome eight-engined aircraft was the largest passenger aircraft in the world. The optimism, sadly, was misplaced and even before a second prototype could be completed it was evident that the future lay with jet airliners; the project was abandoned and the Brabazon scrapped. The Britannia, another graceful aeroplane, soon followed. Powered by four turboprop engines, it enjoyed limited success, but it was the small, ugly, but useful Bristol Freighter which brought commercial success to the company in the field of civil aviation in the 1950s. By the late 1950s it was apparent that the day of the independent aircraft manufacturer was over, and the Bristol Aeroplane Company merged with other leading manufacturers to form the British Aircraft Corporation; in the 1960s the aircraft division was responsible for the British development of Concorde.

Still within the field of transport, the early twentieth century had seen the rise of new firms drawing on the potential of the internal combustion engine. The mid-twentieth century saw their consolidation into important local industries which ensured that, besides aeroplanes, the name Bristol was to become firmly established with cars and motorbikes, buses and lorries. The first motor car had been built in Bristol in 1900 and its builder, Joseph Barter, went on to develop the Douglas motorcycle, which continued in production in Kingswood until the 1950s. Regular car production in the city had to wait until the formation of the car division of the Bristol Aeroplane Company at the end of the Second World War. Drawing from the in-house expertise in aircraft manufacture and from drawings belonging to the German car maker BMW, confiscated after the war, the company entered the field of luxury car production. The first model, the 400, made its debut in 1947 and established the company's reputation for expensive cars which embodied good detailed design, painstaking hand craftsmanship, speed, power, performance, excellent handling and luxury. Buses had been made in Bristol since 1908 when the Bristol Tramways & Carriage Company started their production at Filton for their own use. In 1912 the BT & CC established new works at Brislington and from the 1920s began the production of bus chassis and lorries for sale nationwide. In the late 1930s the company produced nearly 200 new double-decker buses to replace the trams which finally disappeared in 1941. As part of the Tilling Group, the BT & CC was nationalised in 1948, and the following year the Bristol works introduced the Lodekka, a low-height double-decker which enjoyed widespread use with other nationalised bus companies.

Bristol has a long association with the non-ferrous metal industries, particularly lead working and the making of brass. While brass making finally ended in 1927 with the closure of the works at Keynsham, a new industry – zinc smelting – had started ten years earlier at Avonmouth. The works had been established during the First World War to manufacture poisonous gas but had not been completed before the end of hostilities, and in peacetime they were taken over by the National Smelting Company who commenced zinc smelting and the production of sulphuric acid. Subsequently controlled by the Imperial Smelting Corporation and the Consolidated Zinc Corporation, the undertaking experienced continuous growth throughout the mid-twentieth century, including a programme of modernisation and expansion launched in 1965 in collaboration with Imperial Chemical Industries and Fisons.

The rise of new industries was accompanied by the creation of new industrial zones on the edge of the city. The Bristol Aeroplane Company made Filton an industrial area, while the establishment of the BT & CC's works at Brislington in 1912 was followed by the development of an industrial estate along the Bath Road in the 1920s. An industrial estate was developed in Fishponds and after the war the City Council created a trading estate for light industry in Bedminster. These new industrial zones reflected the diminishing influence of the port in determining the location of new factories. Aeroplane production, for example, existed independently of the port; what was important, however, was the availability of cheap land and the presence of good

Shot Tower, Redcliff Hill, 1940s. The shot tower was built in about 1782 by William Watts, a plumber, who patented a new method of making lead shot in 1782 which apparently came to him in a dream. By Watts' patent, the molten lead was dropped from the top of the tower into a vat of cold water where the droplets solidified into near perfect small balls. Watts' patent completely superseded the old method of casting shot in moulds. The tower survived until 1968, when it was demolished for the widening of Redcliff Hill, but Sheldon Bush and Patent Shot Co., owners of the tower since 1868, continue production in Cheese Lane.

communications by road and rail. The Bristol Aeroplane Company's site at Filton was huge, and after the Second World War even swallowed up the village of Charlton to make way for the new runway required for the Brabazon project.

The development of the industrial estate at Avonmouth was again stimulated by the availability of cheap land and good communications, but also reflected the ability of the port to continue to attract industry. Factory sites adjacent to the quaysides had the advantage that bulky raw materials could be processed with the minimum of movement. As the economic role of the City Docks waned so the attraction of Avonmouth increased, and from the 1920s the Port Authority promoted the Avonmouth Docks Trading Estate at Chittening. Flour milling was gradually concentrated in the docks at Avonmouth, while the metallurgical, chemical and petrochemical industries sustained by imported ores and petroleum were largely responsible for the expansion of the Avonmouth industrial zone northwards along the Severn. The rawness of this industrial development, including the vast works of the National Smelting Company on St Andrew's Road, was emphasised by the survival of small farms such as Rockingham, Chittening and Madam farms immediately outside the factory perimeters.

The city centre, meanwhile, which had traditionally had a strong industrial character owing to the presence of the docks, gradually lost some of its industry during this period. Fry's made the decision to leave the centre in 1922. Their factories were hemmed in on all sides preventing further expansion and there were no direct rail or water communications. They chose a 220-acre site in open country at Keynsham with good communications which they named Somerdale. The move was completed by 1931. Some industries in the centre quietly declined and closed while others, such as Price Powell & Co., stoneware manufacturers in St Thomas Street, were destroyed by German bombing. In the post-war period the granaries and mills in the city closed as the industry consolidated its operations at Avonmouth.

In the post-war period more old-established Bristol industries closed or found their local identity greatly reduced. J.S. Fry & Sons had merged their financial interests with Cadbury's as early as 1918 as a response to intense competition in the industry, and in 1935 became a subsidiary of Cadbury's. Bristol's largest soap manufacturer, Christopher Thomas & Brothers, had been taken over by Lever Brothers in 1913; they were well known locally for the Puritan brand of soap but finally ceased production in 1953. This was not quite the end of Bristol's soap and candle-making industry, however, as Carwardines of Sheene Road, Bedminster, remained in business until about 1961. Locomotive building in Bristol – which had always been on a modest scale compared with Manchester, Leeds or Glasgow – finally came to an end with the closure of Peckett's Atlas works in St George in 1962. The closure of Pountney's Bristol Pottery in Fishponds in 1969 marked the end of a centuries-old Bristol industry. Other industries, meanwhile, thrived: Wills maintained their pre-eminence in cigarette production into the 1960s by relaunching the Embassy brand with gift coupons, which were extremely popular. By the 1960s Robinsons, as part of the Dickinson Robinson Group, had become an international packaging and engineering group. The Bristol Motor Car Company bucked the trend towards absorption, surviving the creation of the British Aircraft Corporation in 1961, when it was bought by Sir George White: production continued, with the Bristol 411 appearing in 1969, although from 1961 they were powered by Chrysler engines made in Canada.

Whatever the shifting fortunes of companies at board level, the prime consideration for thousands of ordinary Bristolians was that local industry meant employment and security. Working conditions varied: some workers endured low pay, long hours and hazardous working conditions. Wills and Fry's, on the other hand, had good reputations in spite of strict and paternalistic regimes on the factory floor. The aim of many young people in Bedminster was to find employment with one of the large firms such as Wills, Robinsons or Mardons. At Wills women would traditionally leave the company upon marrying but there were many employees who spent their entire working lives there. From the 1920s women increasingly found opportunities for office employment, a legacy of the First World War, when they had taken the place of men called to the Front. The larger firms generally had good facilities for their employees: each of the Wills factories had a medical room, treatment room and recreational facilities, including athletic grounds and an evening club in Luckwell Road.

Between 1920 and 1969, several major changes to Bristol's industrial structure occurred. Several industries, including soap and glass manufacture, coal mining and potteries disappeared; ship building ended a few years later with the closure of the Albion yard in the City Docks in 1977 and the clothing and footwear industries diminished in importance. Other industries, however, continued to maintain a strong presence in the city – tobacco, printing and packaging, for example – while new industries such as aircraft production and chemical processing expanded. The rise of manufacturing zones at Avonmouth and Severnside, Filton and Brislington marked the decreasing importance of industry to the city centre. As firms merged, the local identity of the city's manufactures was reduced. By 1969, the influence of the Port on determining the siting of new factories was less important than Bristol's new links by motorway with London, South Wales, the Midlands and the South West. This was a factor in the growth of the service sector, including banking and insurance from the 1960s, a trend which continued through the 1970s and 1980s. As the service sector increased in importance, the number of jobs in manufacturing declined. Traditional skills in engineering and other trades and insustries disappeared and high-rise office blocks – not factories – came to dominate the city centre.

Farriers at work at Firash, wheelwrights and farriers, St Thomas Street, October 1937. Many traditional handcrafts survived in Bristol into the 1920s and 1930s but declined after the war. In this view a smith operates the bellows while a horshoe is heated in the forge.

Assembling a wheel at Firash, October 1937. The wheelwright is hammering a felloe (a section of the rim of the wheel) on to the spokes; resting on the nave (the hub) are the remaining two felloes needed to complete the wheel.

Shattock & Hunter, saddlers, Frogmore Street, *c.* 1937. Leather working was traditionally an important trade in the city. Shattock & Hunter were located close to the centre and made saddlery, horse collars, hames and other items of harness.

Byrt Brothers, Netham Cooperage, Redfield, Bristol, *c.* 1937. A beautifully lit photograph inside the Netham cooperage showing a cooper pulling the staves of a barrel together. There was a large demand for barrels in Bristol and in the mid-1930s there were sixteen coopers at work in the city; by 1968–9 only Byrt Brothers survived, and they had gone by 1970.

Basketing jars at Price Powell & Co., Thomas Street Pottery, *c.* 1937. The company formerly had as many as thirty basket-makers at work making basket-ware covers to protect the large wine and spirit jars made for the Christmas trade. Price's made a wide range of functional stoneware products including bottles and jars for cider, soft drinks and ink.

Gervase Thorne throwing a two-gallon stoneware bottle at Price's, *c.* 1937. A foreman potter, Thorne had worked for the company for fifty years. Stoneware manufacture had flourished in the city since the early eighteenth century; Price's business dated to 1796 but came to an abrupt end when their works were bombed in November 1940.

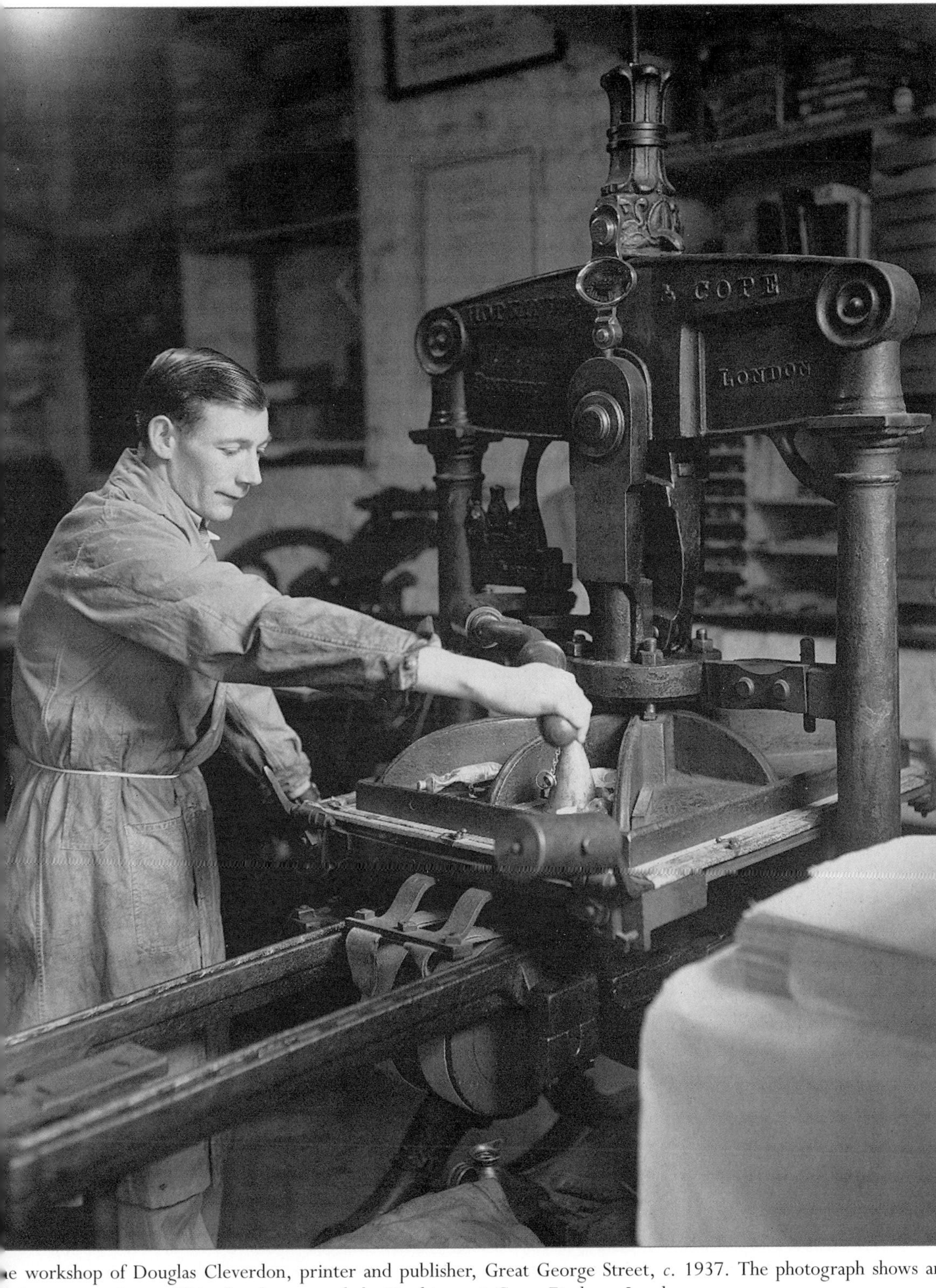

ıe workshop of Douglas Cleverdon, printer and publisher, Great George Street, *c.* 1937. The photograph shows an ıployee operating an Albion hand press made by Hopkinson & Cope, Finsbury, London.

William Terrell & Sons' rope works at Brislington, 1930s. Terrell's were established at Welsh Back in the 1820s, moving to Canon's Marsh in the 1880s and to a new works at Brislington in 1902. They made all sizes of rope up to 4-in hawsers and also held the contract for braided piston packing for locomotives of the Great Western Railway. They were taken over by British Ropes in 1964 and closed the following year.

Hutchings & Skewes Brothers, tailors, 85 Park Street, *c.* 1937. The photograph shows the tailor sitting cross-legged ironing the lapel of a jacket. In the foreground is a sleeve board and in the background numerous tailors' dummies.

nry Simmons Ltd, hatters, 12 St James Barton, *c.* 1937. Bristol was well known for hat making in the nineteenth ntury although the industry was in decline by the 1920s. In 1940 Simmons were advertising themselves as nufacturers of uniform hats and caps, hand-made bowlers and silk top hats. George Ewens, who is seen here, worked Simmons and was the last top hat maker in Bristol. He is seen applying the plush silk covering to the calico foundation means of a hot iron.

The Board of Directors of J.S. Fry & Sons pose for the camera in the board room of the company's Union Street premises in 1928, the bicentenary year, sitting under a portrait of Joseph Storrs Fry (1826–1913). C.R. Fry, sixth in descent from Joseph Fry (1728–87), founder of the firm, is second from the right and E. Cadbury is on the right.

Nut roasting at Fry's, Somerdale, Keynsham, 1932. Roasting the cocoa beans was the first process in the making of either cocoa or chocolate. It was a delicate process requiring skill and careful judgement, as the quality and aromatic flavour of the finished product depended upon the success of this operation. The roasters at Somerdale consisted of huge revolving ovens, which could hold about half a ton of beans and were heated by gas.

Fry's Easter egg and novelty catalogue for Easter 1934. On the cover chicks march out of the new factory site at Somerdale, Keynsham, developed in the 1920s. Until the early 1970s Fry's produced catalogues every year advertising a wide range of fancy chocolates for Easter and Christmas, to supplement their staple range of Five Boys, Turkish Delight, Crunchie, Fry's Cream Bars and drinking cocoas.

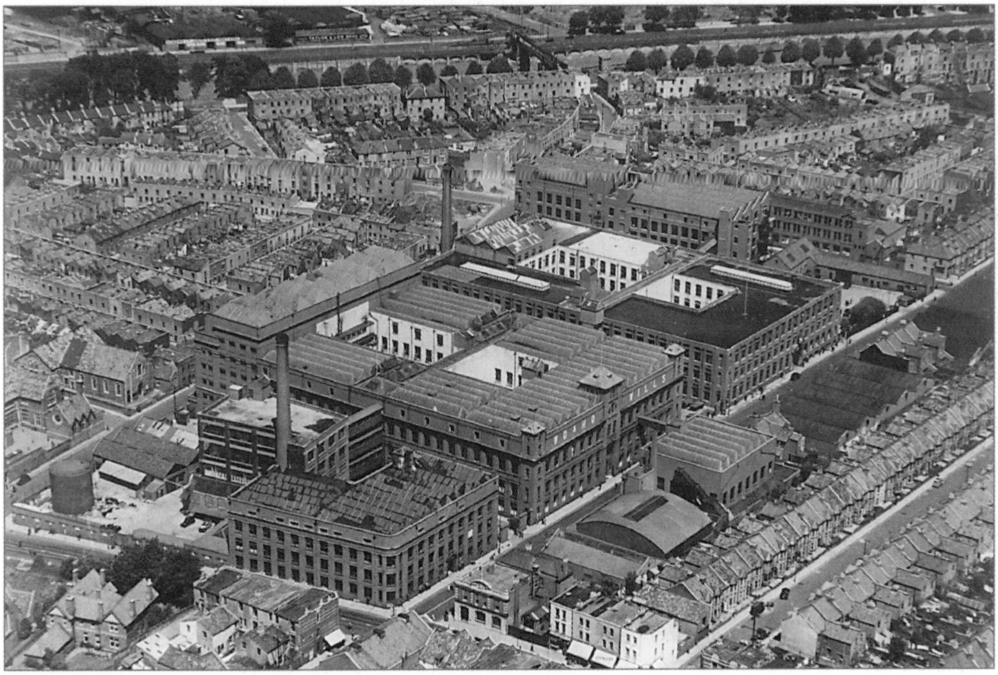

Aerial view of W.D. & H.O. Wills' factories in Raleigh Road towering over the neighbouring streets, *c.* 1950.

Many famous brands of tobacco, cigarettes and cigars have been produced by Wills: Golden Virginia has long maintained the position as the leading handrolling tobacco. The first cigarette brand was Bristol, introduced in 1871. Three Castles appeared in 1878 and Woodbine, which for years was Britain's most popular cigarette, was introduced in 1888. Cigarette cards, printed by Mardons, were originally introduced as packet stiffeners in 1878 and remained popular until 1939. Embassy was introduced in 1914 and was successfully relaunched in 1962 as a coupon cigarette. The coupons were very popular, and within three years had helped Wills achieve nearly 40 per cent of the UK cigarette market by weight and 34 per cent by count: one in four cigarettes sold was an Embassy brand.

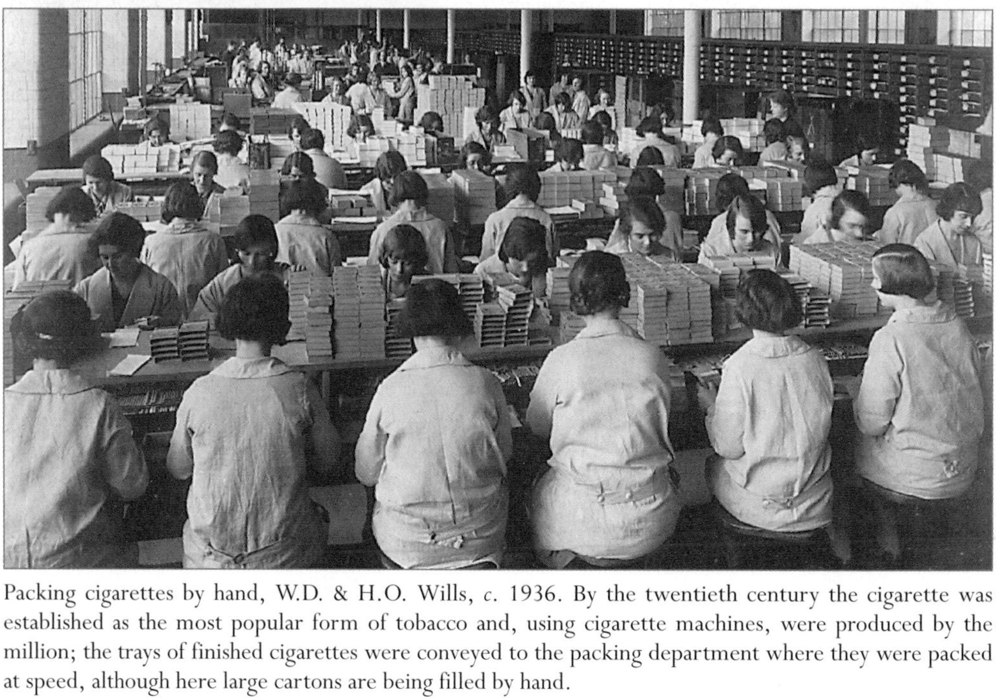

Packing cigarettes by hand, W.D. & H.O. Wills, *c.* 1936. By the twentieth century the cigarette was established as the most popular form of tobacco and, using cigarette machines, were produced by the million; the trays of finished cigarettes were conveyed to the packing department where they were packed at speed, although here large cartons are being filled by hand.

John Harvey inspecting by candlelight a commemorative magnum of Bristol Cream sherry produced for the 1953 coronation; the bottles, which are being filled from a hand bottling machine, were held against the candlelight to ensure that the wine was clear. This was Harvey's first commemorative bottling, and the bottles were given a special label bearing the Queen's monogram.

The Bristol Brabazon (G-AGPW) under construction in its specially built hanger at Filton in about 1947. This aircraft was named after Lord Brabazon, chairman of a committee set up in 1942 to consider Britain's post-war aviation needs, and was developed as a trans-oceanic airliner capable of flying non-stop between London and New York. When it made its maiden flight on 4 September 1949 it was the world's largest civil aeroplane, but in 1952 the project was cancelled – and this prototype was scrapped the following year.

Bristol 170 Freighter, *c.* 1950. This aircraft originated as a military freighter towards the end of the war, and the prototype flew on 2 December 1945. It was developed through several variants, most of which had the large nose doors for ease of freight loading, although the 'Wayfarer' seen here was an all-passenger version built without this feature. Altogether 214 Bristol Freighters were built, and for some twenty-five years this noisy, ungainly but useful aircraft was a familiar sight in British airspace.

Bristol type 401 saloon at the Clifton Suspension Bridge, *c.* 1950. This carefully posed shot of the latest product of the car division of the Bristol Aeroplane Group under the massive chain links of Brunel's suspension bridge shows two contrasting Bristol engineering achievements that were a century apart. The 401 was introduced in the autumn of 1949 as a four-seater two-door saloon; drawing on the company's expertise in aircraft design it was one of the most aerodynamically efficient cars of its time. Production continued until 1953, by which time 650 had been made.

Engine fitter at work on a bus chassis, Bristol Commercial Vehicles, Brislington, 1937. A particular feature of bus production was that the manufacture of the chassis and the bodywork were undertaken separately. Bristol-made bus chassis carried bodies made by several different companies including Easton Coach Works. The works closed in 1983.

Smith's Potato Crisps factory, Bath Road, Brislington, *c.* 1935. This trading estate was developed from the 1920s with some stylish factories facing the A4.

Puritan soap packet by Christopher Thomas & Brothers, Broad Plain, *c.* 1950. The company was founded in 1825 and Puritan bar soap introduced in 1898. In the 1920s and 1930s gift coupons were issued with Puritan soap, and from 1936 until the scheme was withdrawn in 1939 the company had a gift shop in St Augustine's Parade.

CHAPTER THREE

THE CITY CENTRE

Between 1920 and 1969 Bristol's city centre experienced a radical transformation – radical enough, as the photographic record illustrates, to render large parts of the centre of the 1920s and 1930s unrecognisable by the 1960s. The pre-war city centre had changed little since the late nineteenth century when St Augustine's Bridge at the head of the Frome was built, the Tramway Centre established and several important street schemes, such as the extension of Baldwin Street, completed. Then came the war. The blitz caused the destruction of many familiar and much-loved landmarks like the timber-framed Dutch House; several churches were badly damaged and the main shopping centre along Wine Street and Castle Street largely reduced to a desolate bomb site. The subsequent comprehensive replanning – notably the relocation of the shopping centre at Broadmead – marked a break with the past, but some important changes to the city centre had started before the war, particularly in response to a perceived need to provide the city with a new, larger council building in a more dignified setting – and also to deal with the greatest problem of all: traffic.

The role of the City's planners, engineers and some architects in grappling with the problems of adapting an old city centre to the requirements of the twentieth century exposed the deep differences that can exist between professional and popular opinion. The planners came to regard the densely packed pre-war centre as a monument to the 'mistakes of the past'. The city, they saw, lacked a focus – the jumble of Georgian and Victorian buildings lining the Frome unworthy of a large and important city. They saw Bristol's city centre as a place of appalling chaos: overcrowded housing, shops, offices, churches and factories compressed along narrow roads congested with traffic; and a centre that also lacked open space.

The congestion could not be doubted: in 1934 J.B. Priestley described the centre of Bristol with some affection as 'a place where trams and coastal steamers seemed in danger of a collision'. The centre clearly lacked a formal and symbolic central focus but instead had several that were genuine and practical: the Tramway Centre – a raised triangle of pavement above St Augustine's Bridge where trams (until 1939), buses and taxis provided the physical means of connection between the centre and the suburbs;

Corn Street – which served as the business and commercial heart of the city; and Wine Street and Castle Street further east – which formed the main shopping centre and also a social focus, a place where people promenaded on Saturday and Sunday evenings. The scale was human and intimate, with narrow streets crammed with a wealth of architectural variety – from medieval timber framing to Edwardian baroque in brick and Bath stone. But as J.B. Priestley observed, Bristol had not gone quaint: it was also a busy modern commercial centre, and factory chimneys vied with church spires for prominence on the skyline. And the city was not without its open space: Queen's Square, College Green and several churchyards offered quiet seclusion without detracting from the overall cohesion of the cityscape; but these were not the wide-open formal spaces which the planners desired.

The inadequacy of the old Council House had been apparent since the early 1900s, and in 1919 the City set up a special committee to consider a scheme for acquiring a site for municipal buildings on College Green. Progress was slow, and it was not until 1933 that E. Vincent Harris was appointed architect of the scheme. The designs were approved the following year, and in 1935 old property on College Green was demolished to make way for the site and the foundation stone was laid. By the outbreak of war the building was largely completed. Harris had designed a long, curved neo-Georgian building facing the city centre. It is a sombre, dignified building, but has attracted criticism for the preponderance of the hipped roof and for its unusual domed central porch. The Council decided to use pale brown hand-made bricks from Moreton-in-Marsh, Gloucestershire, as the principal facing material so that the importance of the cathedral should not be challenged. This sensitivity to the immediate surroundings contrasts with the decision taken after the war to lower the level of College Green in response to the architect's request that it would 'make' his building; unfortunately the felling of the mature trees together with the removal of the railings and the replica high cross has been widely condemned, creating in the words of Professor J.V. Punter 'a billiard table wasteland of flat lawns and aimless paths'.

The problem of traffic congestion was not new. In the second half of the nineteenth century several important changes were made to routes through the centre to ease the flow of traffic. What was new after 1920 was the rise in private ownership of the motor car: between the end of the First World War and 1930 the number of cars in Britain increased from about 200,000 to over one million. Congestion worsened and motorists began complaining about the shortage of places to park. Bristol was the meeting place of eleven main roads, including two national routes which intersected at St Augustine's Parade: the A4 linking Avonmouth with London and the A38 from the Midlands to the south-west. In 1936 the City began work on the creation of an inner circuit road intended to link the major routes and thus lessen the volume of traffic in the centre. A new thoroughfare, Temple Way, cut a new course to the south from Old Market towards Temple Meads, crossing the Floating Harbour by a new bridge at Temple Back. The route continued westwards into Redcliffe Way. Here the road ran close to the north porch of St Mary Redcliffe and caused the demolition of the corner of Pile Street and St Thomas Street. After crossing the docks by a new bridge the road then cut diagonally across Queen Square, effectively destroying the peace and tranquillity of this eighteenth-century square and leaving Rysbrack's equestrian statue of William III stranded on a central traffic island. Beyond the square, where the road met Prince Street and King Street, a roundabout was built which involved the demolition of the Merchants Arms public house. In the centre the flow of traffic between Redcliffe Way and College Green was simplified by covering in a stretch of the Frome below St Augustine's Bridge. This modification transformed the centre: Broad Quay lost its waterfront and the shops on St Augustines Parade no longer looked over to ships. Effectively, Bristol's 'street of ships' had disappeared – and all of this was completed before the first bomb fell on Bristol.

The Blitz during the evening of 24 November 1940 caused widespread devastation to Bristol. In the centre it wiped out much of Wine Street and Castle Street. Mary-le-Port Street, a quaint, narrow thoroughfare, was destroyed; so too was the Dutch House – a much photographed timber-framed house on the corner of Wine Street and the High Street – and, saddest of all, St Peter's Hospital, a fifteenth-century merchant's house (see *Bristol 1850–1919*, page 108). There were more losses over the ensuing months. Many Bristolians, it is clear, felt disorientation and a deep sense of loss at the destruction of familiar surroundings, but the planners saw things differently. The clearing of the site by enemy bombs, in their view, enormously simplified the problem and provided a unique opportunity to replan the centre.

In 1942 a Planning and Reconstruction Committee was created by the City, and two years later released plans for a radical reshaping of the city. The *Evening Post* described them as 'bold beyond the wildest dreams of most people'. Traffic remained a prime consideration (the City Engineer recommended the addition of an inner ring road to intercept the major radial roads), but the most radical idea was the creation of separate zones for civic use, shopping and education in place of the former mixture and diversity of land use in the centre. Thus a large tract of land was set aside on St Michael's Hill and Kingsdown for the expansion of the university on the western side and the hospitals to the east. The Wine Street/Castle Street area was to become a new cultural centre with a concert hall, museum and art gallery, while the shopping centre was to be relocated to a new site at Broadmead. Industry would be moved to new sites in the suburbs where factories, housing, schools and recreational facilities would be grouped in 'neighbourhood units'.

The relocation of the shopping centre to Broadmead was the suggestion that caused greatest concern. Wine Street and Castle Street formed a popular and valuable shopping centre linking east and west Bristol, and it was felt by many that removing the shops would result in the sterilisation of a large and important area in the heart of the city. The traders were anxious to resume business there as soon as possible: Broadmead was off the beaten track in their view, and the support of the multiple traders for Broadmead (their major competitors) only strengthened their opposition. A poll of shoppers organised by the Bristol Retail Trades Federation in 1947 demonstrated overwhelming support for the old shopping centre: 13,363 votes in favour as opposed to 418 votes for Broadmead. The government response was also lukewarm. The City's grand vision, they considered, was inappropriate in a climate of austerity, and in 1947 the Government cut Bristol's redevelopment plans.

The City, however, was adamant that Broadmead was the better option – offering a less restricted site where shops would benefit from wider frontages. So they pressed ahead, albeit with a much reduced plan. The decision to demolish the Lower Arcade was reversed in response to protests from the Council for the Protection of Ancient Bristol and others. But the more fundamental objections to the Broadmead scheme voiced by local traders and architects were largely ignored. In 1952 Sir John Inskip, Chairman of the Planning and Reconstruction Committee, confidently asserted: 'I picture Broadmead during the next few years a hive of building activity and within the coming decade a vista of pleasant shops and do I hear some of our present-day critics saying, "they were right"?' The arrogance of local politicians, their failure to involve interested parties in the decision-making process and the compulsory land purchases enforced in Broadmead created a deep feeling of antipathy from a wide section of the Bristol public towards the City Council – and their new shopping centre.

Broadmead, a council shopping estate, exhibited the same dull uniformity that characterised its housing estates. The retention of the Greyhound Hotel, Quakers' Friars and the Lower Arcade provided some degree of visual relief but generally the new shopping centre lacked the variety and character of the old. The City Architect wished for 'good, simple and dignified architecture', but most of the new shops were bland in the extreme. And, paradoxically, while the City treated the smaller traders in an arbitrary and high-handed manner it readily capitulated to the demands of the more powerful multiple companies, many of whom used their own in-house architects to design their stores and, like Woolworths, insisted on their standard fascias. By 1954 the first phase of Broadmead and Union Street was complete. The next phase saw new shops introduced as far as Penn Street by 1956, resulting in the demolition of old property in Merchant Street and the total eradication of Old King Street, Rosemary Street and Milk Street from the city centre map. Many old buildings, including several public houses, disappeared. The third phase, which took the number of shops in Broadmead to a total of 148, extended as far as Broad Weir and the Inner Circuit Road and was completed by 1960. Dull and characterless, deserted after 6.00 pm in the evenings, Broadmead failed to provide the new focus that the planners had hoped for. The old shopping centre, meanwhile, remained a desolate wasteland – a vacuum in the heart of the city – as plans for the new civic and cultural centre were postponed as the Council turned to the more pressing need to provide new housing.

Beyond Broadmead, other developments were to pull apart the old centre and its immediate surroundings and destroy its coherence. In response to the 1947 Town & Country Planning Act, which required local authorities to produce plans and take control of new development, the City Council published its first Development Plan in 1952. For the central area this involved the completion of the Inner Circuit Road from Old Market to St James's Barton and thence via Bond Street and Lewins Mead to Colston Avenue. Completion of this in the 1950s and 1960s cut a swathe through old Bristol north and west of the Broadmead shopping centre: streets were realigned and widened, and shops and many historic buildings disappeared as considerations of traffic flow outweighed any sentiment for the past. The plan also sanctioned the development of university and hospital extensions in Kingsdown, and here from the mid-1950s large parts of this picturesque Georgian suburb were destroyed to make way for new university and hospital buildings. Similarly, the development of a new entertainment complex in Frogmore Street in the mid-1960s resulted in the large-scale demolition of a maze of picturesque old streets and lanes overlooking the centre. Within the centre itself much of the City's radical vision disintegrated under waves of office developments, over which the Council exerted, at best, weak and vacillating control.

From about 1959 until the early 1970s the centre fell victim to a boom in office building, which coincided with a vogue for high-rise towers and blocks. Within the space of a few years the historic city skyline – a harmonious mix of church towers, spires and cupolas, rooftops and chimneys of many varieties which had taken centuries to evolve – was ruined. Bristol's first post-war office building, Gaunt's House, overlooking College Green, was completed in 1952; this steel-framed block faced in Bath stone anticipated subsequent office developments, not only in the method of construction but also the way in which the sheer bulk of the building dwarfed its immediate surroundings, including the Lord Mayor's chapel; it also paid scant regard to the medieval street plan. In 1961 the Council released land on the corner of the High Street and Wine Street earmarked for civic use – to an insurance company and the Bank of England. Despite strong public opposition the construction of the Norwich Union building and the Bank of England went ahead, but the two buildings failed miserably to do justice to this prominent site in the heart of the old medieval city.

Much of the office building in the mid-1960s was speculative, fuelled by the 22 per cent increase in growth of the service sector in Bristol between 1961 and 1969. Nevertheless, the first office block to have a major impact on the city centre skyline belonged to a company with strong local roots: this was the fifteen-storey Robinson building built on the site of their Victorian premises near Bristol Bridge in 1965. At the time of its construction this tower block, over 200 ft tall, was considerably higher than anything else in the city centre, and while the façades exhibited careful detailed design the building still jarred with its immediate surroundings through its sheer size and the choice of white pre-cast concrete as the facing material. In the absence of a high buildings policy from the Council – who themselves were building high-rise blocks of flats across the city at this time – other tall blocks in the centre soon followed: Tower House in Fairfax Street, the South West Regional Government offices in the Pithay, occupying a commanding site on the centre, the Bristol & West building, and St Lawrence House, twelve storeys high, which towered over the neighbouring spire of St John's-in-the-Wall. The intrusion of these drab, dreary blocks of concrete and glass within a relatively short period took place to mounting criticism, especially as some of them replaced fine Victorian and Edwardian commercial buildings.

In 1966 the City Council published a Development Plan Review. It was dominated by a spirit of uncompromising modernism: there was no high buildings policy, despite mounting pressure for one. Highway schemes still dominated the planners' thinking, and it was these which caused the greatest opposition. Traffic congestion continued to grow as car ownership in Bristol continued to rise: in 1948 there were 20,000 private car owners in the city, and between 1950 and 1961 car ownership doubled. The free circulation of traffic was seen as the greatest priority and the Review proposed a vertical segregation of road traffic and pedestrians in the centre by creating pedestrian decks above the roads, while an outer circuit road would intercept incoming traffic. The plans required the comprehensive redevelopment of large tracts of central Bristol, while the road system would have resulted in laying waste large parts of the inner suburbs. Work on the outer circuit road began, cutting a swathe through Easton and resulting in the demolition of 550 houses in Totterdown, but that was as far as the new road system got. By 1973 the plan was rendered obsolete by a fundamental shift in national policy on urban road schemes – a response to growing concern for the environmental consequences of urban roads. The same year saw the collapse of the commercial property market and the end of the era of slab and tower office building. When the property market recovered in the late 1970s the climate of opinion had undergone a fundamental shift: planners came to see the merits of conservation and public consultation, and taking public opinion into account became an integral part of the planning process. Modernism was out of fashion and the primacy of motor traffic was no longer taken for granted, but together the Blitz and mid-twentieth-century planning philosophies have left their indelible mark on Bristol's city centre.

e view down Broad Street to St John's Gateway from the Grand Hotel, early 1930s: a picturesque roof top view of the y centre on a sunny morning before the scene was altered by post-war developments. There is a strong flavour of thic architecture to the scene, with the roof of the Guildhall in the centre. Designed by the Bristol architect, Richard ackleton Pope, in the Perpendicular style, the Guildhall was built in 1843 to provide more suitable accommodation for courts, but from the first was criticised because of its inadequacy and inconvenience. Broad Street ends at St John's teway, the only medieval gateway in the city wall to survive, which supports the fourteenth-century tower and spire of John's church. To the right of the spire, in the distance, St Michael's church in Kingsdown can be seen. The photograph s taken before Electricity House was built on a site bounded by Rupert Street, Nelson Street and Christmas Street; signed by Sir Giles Scott, the building was begun in 1936 and completed after the war.

Three familiar Bristol landmarks punctuate the skyline: on the left is Cabot Tower, built to commemorate the 400th niversary of the discovery of Newfoundland by John Cabot who sailed from Bristol; to the right is the tower of the lls university building, designed by Sir George Oatley; and further right again is the square gothic block of the Physics ilding of 1929, which was also the work of Oatley. Also dating to 1929 but of a very different character is the bright, odernistic Northcliffe House, centre left, premises of the *Evening World* in Colston Avenue. After the war the ngsdown hillside overlooking the centre was unsympathetically developed with hospital and university extensions, ile St John's church was dwarfed by St Lawrence House, a large office block built in 1967.

St John's Gateway, 1920s. The view of Broad Street looking through St John's Gateway has been a popular subject with photographers ever since the early days of photography in the 1850s. The Grand Hotel built in 1868 is on the left in front of Christ Church. The timber-framed Dutch House can just be glimpsed on the corner of Wine Street and the High Street.

Martins Bank, on the corner of Corn Street and Small Street, late 1930s. This handsome classical building in the commercial heart of Bristol was designed by James Weir, a London architect, and was built by the London and South Western Bank on the site of St Werburgh's church. The church was demolished in 1878 and the banking house opened in 1880; it is now a Wetherspoon's pub.

Corn Street, 1930s: a pre-war view of the east end of Corn Street, with the Dutch House visible on the corner of the High Street. The tower of All Saints' church was added by William Paul and George Townsend between 1712 and 1717 and the cupola by Luke Henwood in 1807. On the right is the imposing Palladian façade of the Exchange built in 1741–3 to the design of John Wood; the Coffee House alongside was designed by Thomas Paty in 1782.

The Dutch House, corner of Wine Street and High Street, *c.* 1930. This merchant's house of 1676 was a well-known city centre landmark, and in the 1920s and 1930s was occupied by the Irish Linen and Hosiery Association. It was damaged beyond repair in the air raid of 24 November 1940, and in 1964 the Bank of England building was built on the site.

Host Street, 1930s. A dramatic, night-time view of sixteenth-century timber-framed houses in Host Street illuminated, it would seem, by floodlights. They contained a well-known fried fish shop and a medieval arch, a fragment of St Bartholomew's Hospital, founded before 1207.

No. 33 King Street from the corner of King William Street, *c.* 1930. King Street, immediately south of the city walls, was laid out in about 1650–60 and named by a loyal Corporation in celebration of the Restoration of King Charles II in 1660. This timber-framed gabled house of the late seventeenth century is crammed in between nineteenth-century warehouses, and contains a section of the old city wall in its structure.

The corner of Union Street and Nelson Street, 1936. Fry's imposing granite and brick corner office block was demolished early in 1937 and replaced by the Odeon Cinema, which opened in June 1938.

Fry's factory no. 7, corner of Tower Lane and the Pithay, 6 February 1938. Designed by Sir George Oatley and built in 1905, this factory was made redundant when Fry's moved to Keynsham. After serving as Her Majesty's Stationery Office, it was demolished in 1964 to make way for Pithay House, an office block belonging to Capital & Counties. The Cadena café was one of several in the city from about 1909, and the Prince of Wales was one of the many George's pubs in the city.

The Frome under Union Street, 1936. The course of the River Frome is marked by the low-roofed offices belonging to J.S. Fry's, in a yard which is occupied by the present-day route of Fairfax Street. Fry's factories loom over the space on the left, while the large brick building on the right of the steps leading up to Union Street belonged to Ferris & Co., wholesale druggists, established 1754. Smart Brothers' furnishing store is across the road on the corner of Union Street and Fairfax Street, which follows the line of the river into the distance.

Union Street, 1936. This was photographed shortly before the Fry's showrooms and offices on the left were demolished and replaced by the Odeon cinema and new shops.

The newly completed Union Street Bridge, *c*. 1953.

Union Street, 21 August 1938. Fry's new showrooms maintain the presence of the firm in Union Street, which dated from 1777. On the corner is the new Odeon cinema, designed by T. Cecil Howitt, which had opened the previous month.

Upper Arcade, *c.* 1950. Designed by James Foster and built in 1824, the Upper Arcade ran between St James's Barton and the Horsefair. It was destroyed by bombing in 1940, and in this view, taken before the ruins were cleared for new shops in Broadmead, the Ionic columns of the entrance frame 12 St James's Barton, an impressive house of 1728 that was demolished in 1960.

City centre bomb site, *c.* 1950. Cellars of buildings destroyed in the Blitz below the ruins of St Peter's church provide extra parking in the heart of the pre-war shopping centre. In 1944 this area was zoned for civic use by the City Council's Planning and Reconstruction Committee, but the plans were first delayed and then abandoned.

Milk Street, *c.* 1950. Two public houses are seen here – the Lamb & Anchor and the Crown & Cushion. Both dated to at least the late eighteenth century, being listed in Mathew's Bristol Directory for 1794, but they were demolished along with the rest of the street in the mid-1950s to make way for the building of the second phase of the Broadmead shopping centre.

Rosemary Street, *c.* 1950. These Georgian houses were demolished in about 1954 and the street disappeared under an eastern extension of Broadmead beyond Merchant Street.

Offices and works of E.S. & A. Robinson Ltd, cardboard box and paper bag manufacturers, near Bristol Bridge in Victoria Street shortly before demolition in 1961. This imposing brick building was designed by William Bruce Gingell and built in 1876. The building had a chequered history, being partially destroyed by fire in 1903 and then badly damaged in the war when the corner tower lost its large dome. Notwithstanding its forlorn appearance, the building preserves the exuberance of Gingell's original design, with a variety of arch patterns and mouldings in brick. The Robinson Group built a fifteen-storey block in its place, which at over 200 ft in height became a dominant city centre landmark.

King Street, *c*. 1961. St Nicholas Almshouses on the corner with Queen Charlotte Street date from 1652. In this view the almshouses are in a poor state of repair; they were renovated during the 1960s but lost something of their character in the process: the tall chimney-stacks and the moulded drip courses above the ground floor windows were removed. The low gabled roof of the almshouses is dwarfed by the Palladian façade of the Cooper's Hall, designed by William Halfpenny. Next again is the Theatre Royal, the oldest playhouse in the country, which opened in 1766.

Lewins Mead looking towards the Horsefair, *c.* 1950. The extension of the Inner Circuit Road through Lewins Mead and 1960s office developments resulted in the removal of much old property, including the Bristol United Breweries (taken over by its local rival George's in 1956) on the left. The brewery was an attractive building with a façade of yellow brick with red string courses. The Fire Brigade station, opened in 1930, is on the right.

The Cathedral and College Green, *c.* 1930: an old-established green bounded by the Cathedral and the Lord Mayor's chapel. In this view the statue of Queen Victoria by Sir J.E. Boehm, erected in 1888 to commemorate her Golden Jubilee in 1887, is seen against a backdrop of trees which were felled between 1950 and 1951 – when College Green was re-landscaped upon the completion of the Council House.

e Tramway Centre from College Green, September 1937. The towers of St Stephen's church, Christ Church, All nts' and shops on Broad Quay reflect the early evening sunshine under a brooding, overcast sky. This view had changed le since St Augustine's Bridge had been built at the head of the culverted Frome in 1893, but work on covering the en section of water seen here had already begun and the Dublin Shed, the port's first transit shed, had been demolished year before; at the time of this photograph its site was serving as a temporary car park (below the Bovril sign). By the nmer of the following year the culvert for the river was well advanced and was completed in 1940. The landscaping of large central island, however, was delayed until after the war.

Three trams can be seen below the trees in Colston Avenue and these will leave the centre for ever in two years' time; e of the double-decker buses which were to replace the trams in large numbers is approaching the camera. Horse-wn traffic, however, remains in evidence and a covered wagon is seen leaving Canon's Road. Neon advertising signs are ticularly prominent on the shops on Broad Quay: the dominance of the giant Bovril sign is testimony to the power of vertising. These signs were a victim of air-raid precautions which involved a nightly 'black-out', and did not reappear er the war. A more conventional sign board on the extreme right of the view advertises Coast Lines Seaway's services all parts of Britain. The telephone box is an early K1 model of pre-cast concrete, first introduced in 1923.

Radiant House, Colston Street, the headquarters of the Bristol Gas Company, was partially rebuilt in the modern-style architecture which began to appear in the city centre after 1930. The new façade with its curved windows – typical of the 1930s – was designed by Whinney Son and Austen Hall and opened on 29 March 1935. The side façade is part of the original 1904 building, designed by William Venn Gough. The building was lit not by gas but by electricity: by 1935 even the gas company had to admit that the future of artificial lighting lay with electricity.

The centre, *c.* 1935–9: a view looking up Colston Street towards the City Council-owned Colston Hall, after the building of Radiant House and before tram services from the centre finished in 1939. The Victorian commercial block on the corner of Colston Street and Colston Avenue was demolished in May 1970 to make way for Colston Tower.

The centre, *c.* 1955: a post-war view of the centre showing the bland elongated roundabout landscaped in 1949 over the section of the Frome culverted between 1938 and 1940. The row of eighteenth- and nineteenth-century buildings on the north side of the centre, which planners in the 1940s had considered unworthy of a city centre, survived, although the Hippodrome lost its revolving dome in 1964.

The centre, *c.* 1965. Traffic roars around the municipal lawns and flower beds of the large traffic island on the centre – not a place of repose but just an obstacle to be crossed by pedestrians (right) as quickly as possible. Modern offices are already changing the cityscape – and the Robinson building rises above the buildings in Baldwin Street. The handsome Atlas and Sun Life building on the corner of Clare Street – a fine example of Edwardian baroque commercial architecture – was replaced in 1971 by a bland office block.

Bridgehead, 24 April 1968. Taken from the Bristol & West building, one of the new city centre landmarks of the 1960s, this view features several important post-war changes to this part of the centre: the landscaping at the head of the Frome with the statue of Neptune, completed in 1949; the Council House presiding over a flat and treeless College Green; and on the right the monolithic block of Gaunt's House, Bristol's first post-war office block, obscuring the tower of the Lord Mayor's chapel. Mid-'60s offices face College Green. The site of St Augustine-the-Less is a patch of derelict land, while the presence of a catamaran in St Augustine's Reach points to the future leisure role of the Floating Harbour.

Chapter Four

Retailing & Victualling

In 1952 there were 7,159 shops in Bristol, one for every sixty-two people in the city. This number embraced a wide range of retailing businesses – from large prestigious department stores such as Baker, Baker & Co. to small corner shops. Roughly one seventh of the total were located in the city centre and reflected the city's role as a regional shopping centre. Another two thousand or so shops were located on the busy main roads leading out of the city, forming six important district shopping centres for the suburbs. They were located on Whiteladies Road including Cotham Hill; Gloucester Road including Cheltenham Road and Filton Road; Stapleton Road and Fishponds Road; Old Market and West Street, extending eastwards to Lawrence Hill and Church Road; Wells Road and Bedminster, with the largest number of shops in North Street followed by East Street and West Street. They contained a comprehensive range of shops including chain stores, banks and building society branches.

Smaller shopping centres were also spread across the suburbs: in Shirehampton, Clifton, Westbury-on-Trym and elsewhere; these were also self-contained shopping centres and included banks and post offices. Scattered throughout the city – particularly in the older suburban districts – small rows of shops and public houses were found, catering for the essential needs of residents in the immediate locality and often characterised by strong personal relationships between shopkeeper and customer. The shops in Whitehouse Street, Bedminster, before the war were a typical example: in 1939 there were two greengrocers, a butcher, boot repairer, a newsagent, grocer's shop, a fried fish shop, and a lamp and oil dealer as well as several general stores. The range, type and distribution of shops in Bristol underwent several important changes during this period, reflecting national changes in retailing – the rise of the chain stores, for example, and adapting to changes in consumer demand in a period of rising standards of living: in the 1920s and 1930s the number of electrical stores and car dealers increased at the expense of some traditional trades such as saddlery, which lost business as the city's horse population declined.

The larger department stores – with the obvious exception of Woolworths where before the war nothing cost more than 6*d* – emphasised their exclusiveness and quality with opulent interiors and enforced a rigid dress code on their staff. In the 1930s assistants employed by Cole & Pottow, high class gentlemen's outfitters in Park Street, changed their attire according to the seasons: in spring they wore a lounge suit with buttonhole; in summer white flannels and a boater; in the autumn they wore plus-fours and a trilby; and in winter a black coat and waistcoat, pin-striped trousers and either a bowler hat or homburg. The shop fronts often incorporated the latest ideas on shop design and advertising: chrome, plate glass and neon lights in the 1930s, large plastic fascias in the 1950s and 1960s.

The smaller shops, in contrast, were often conservative in appearance and preserved late Victorian or Edwardian shop fronts and interiors with lots of tiles, polished brass, wrought-iron work and mosaic floors in the entrance. Typically they were small, family-run concerns and many continued in business over several generations. The furnishings and counter equipment – even the smells – of the different types of shops gave them a distinctive atmosphere and character of their own: bacon waiting to be sliced was the predominant smell in grocery stores, blended, perhaps, with the sweet aroma of biscuits on open display in tins; the tiled interiors and smell of fresh sawdust characterised butchers' shops; while shoe repair shops were permeated with the strong smell of shoe polish and leather. The radio sets, gramophones and, from the 1950s, television sets filled the interior of electrical repair shops with the unmistakable smell emanating from large quantities of bakelite. The interiors of old fashioned chemists' shops – and there were several surviving in the 1960s – in Old Market, West Mall, Clifton and Blackboy Hill, for example – were lined with shelves filled with onion-shaped carboys, large glass bottles used for liquids and cylindrical bottles for solids, known, from their shape, as 'shop rounds'. Ironmongers' shops provided a wide range of household goods and offered a range of practical services such as the installation and repair of items and home decorating; they also had their own distinctive character, with galvanised ware displayed outside on the street and inside a strong smell of paraffin, glue and linseed oil. Many goods were sold loose: nails were sold by the pound and cement and plaster were also sold by weight; similarly, grocers sold many provisions loose. The scoops and counter scales of various kinds used to handle the goods were, in many cases, supplied by the Bristol firm W. Parnall & Co., who before the war had large premises in Victoria Street; they also supplied other shop fittings such as cash tills, display stands and cabinets and window blinds.

Retailing demanded specialised knowledge and skill that could only be acquired through a lengthy apprenticeship. Young assistants in clothes shops would be trained to measure and cut clothes and dress windows. In the ironmongery and hardware business the apprentices would be expected to familiarise themselves with the enormous range of small fixtures and fittings, lamp parts, plumbers' sundries, varnishes and paints. Apprentices in the shoe repair trade would be trained in leather-working techniques using specialised tools, while in the grocery trade assistants would learn to taste and blend teas, slice ham and learn about cheese and other foodstuffs. Shop assistants worked long hours and often on low wages, although many had a half day off on Wednesdays when many shops closed at 1.00 pm. Several small traders provided a delivery service. Besides the daily visit of the milkman, bakers often delivered daily while grocers, greengrocers and butchers made weekly deliveries. All the major retailing trades had their own associations which provided a range of services, including representation to manufacturers, suppliers and to relevant government bodies, and supplied insurance, legal advice and information on wages and holidays.

Shops belonging to the Bristol and District Co-operative Society were widely distributed across Bristol and formed an important and distinctive form of retailing in the city. The society was founded in 1884 by a group of trade unionists with the objective of sharing the profits made through the production and sale of the 'necessaries of life' with members – the consumers – and not just a few shopkeepers. Starting with a shop in St Paul's, branches were opened in Hotwells and Lawrence Hill, and by the mid-1930s there were fifty-two grocery, confectionery and greengrocery branches in Bristol, seven drapery, clothing and boot branches, two hardware and furnishing shops and nineteen butchery branches. There were also shops in nearby towns such as Weston-super-Mare and Clevedon. In 1918 new central premises were established in Castle Street, which opened as a department store in 1930. In 1938 co-operative stores in Britain accounted for 10 per cent of retail trade but the societies saw their role in wider terms. 'Co operation', it was affirmed in the Bristol members' guide for 1934, ' is not merely producing and shopkeeping, it is a method of life.' The Bristol society, for example, had a Women's Guild which educated members in the principles of the movement and on other social issues affecting everyday life. For the majority of members, however, the greatest benefit of society membership was the payment of the dividend – the 'divi' – of 1*s* 8*d* for every £1 spent in the shops.

Before the war the most important and prestigious shops were located in two major shopping centres: the first was the Wine Street/Castle Street area, including Union Street, Dolphin Street, Mary-le-Port Street and Peter Street, where 218 shops were located in 1939. The second major concentration, consisting of 193 shops in 1939, followed the main route to Clifton from College Green to Queens Road via Park Street. In both centres clothes, boot and shoe shops accounted for almost 40 per cent of the total, with food and drink shops the second largest category. Miscellaneous stores included radio shops, such as J. & M. Stone who had shops in Wine Street and Castle Street, Kendall's umbrella shop in Union Street and Halford's cycle store in Castle Street. Two large Bristol department stores – Jones & Co. and Baker, Baker & Co. – had premises in Wine Street where the most exclusive shops were found, and by the 1930s several important multiple traders – Woolworths, Boots, Burtons and Marks & Spencer – were located in Castle Street. The larger chains increased in importance between the wars: nationally between 1920 and 1939 the larger companies with more than 200 branches or more increased from 10,942 to 21,283. The Wine Street/Castle Street shopping centre was busy through the week until the early evening and later on Saturdays, when the shops stayed open until 9.00 pm. On a Saturday night the streets were thronged with people looking for bargains, particularly fresh food (fish, fruit and vegetables) being sold off cheap. Barrow boys, selling fruit and vegetables mostly, were an essential part of the scene with their entertaining banter, their handcarts illuminated by candle lamps on dark evenings.

Enemy bombing destroyed the Wine Street/Castle Street shopping centre: a total of 487 shops were lost in the central area and many traders had to find new premises quickly: an immediate effect was to enhance the importance of the city's radial shopping centres. The City Council ruled out the option of rebuilding shops in Wine Street and Castle Street and instead resolved to develop a new shopping precinct at Broadmead. Despite strong opposition from many local traders and shoppers, the City Council pressed ahead with plans for Broadmead, and the 1950s saw the development of a new shopping precinct which consolidated the hold of the multi-traders at the expense of locally based businesses; moreover, Broadmead never recaptured the atmosphere of the pre-war city centre shopping area. A few shops in Castle Street survived the blitz and lingered on for a while: the Bristol Co-operative Society's headquarters continued in business until the building of Fairfax House in about 1960, and the last shop in Castle Street was Burtons, which survived until 1964.

The pattern of shops in the suburbs also changed in the post-war period. New shopping centres were built on the new post-war housing estates in the 1950s, in Lawrence Weston, Henbury, Stockwood, Withywood and Hartcliffe. At the same time clearances in the older suburbs, such as in Redcliff, parts of Bedminster and St Phillips Marsh, resulted in the closure of many small shops. Thus the small shops in Whitehouse Street, Bedminster, which had thrived before the war, had mostly gone by 1950 as the area was cleared to make way for a light industrial and trading estate. From the late 1950s the small shopkeepers, particularly grocers and general corner shops, found themselves facing a new rival – the supermarket. The development of large self-service stores was a gradual one which began in the 1950s, with some of the larger

Shop window display, Mumford's grocery store, 11 High Street, Westbury-on-Trym, 1951. This window arrangement featuring coffee was inspired by Alma Cogan's song 'Coffee in the Morning'. It was entered for a shop window competition organised by the Bristol & District Grocers' & Provision Dealers' Association which represented the grocery trade in Bristol from 1891 until 1992, when it was dissolved following a decline in membership.

grocery companies such as the Bristol Co-operative Society turning to this method of retailing. Supermarkets first acquired a separate entry in Kelly's Directory in 1964. By the end of the decade there were nearly sixty supermarkets in Bristol and they had successfully gained a foothold in most of the city's suburban shopping centres, some of them occupying former cinemas, such as the Cabot in Filton and the Ritz in Brislington, which found a new lease of life as a Kwik Save store. In 1969 there were seventeen Co-operative supermarkets in Bristol, twenty-three belonging to Gateway and a smaller number of self-service stores owned by Tesco, International, Spar and Fine Fare. The small independently owned stores could not compete with supermarket prices – and, perhaps, the novelty and convenience of shopping in supermarkets – and began to decline in numbers. Notwithstanding the expansion of Bristol between 1920 and 1969, numbers of butchers and grocers – two staple food shops – declined over this period: in 1920 there were some 550 grocers (excluding Bristol Co-operative Society Shops) in Bristol, but by 1969 the figure had dropped to about 420; while numbers of butchers' shops decreased slightly, from roughly 270 in 1920 to about 250 in 1969.

In 1920 there were 371 public houses in Bristol. Some were of considerable antiquity: the Shakespeare in Temple Street was claimed as Bristol's oldest hostelry, possibly dating to 1636. Other old inns included the Greyhound Hotel in Broadmead, the Hatchet Inn in Frogmore Street and the Llandoger Trow, where Daniel Defoe apparently met Alexander Selkirk, the inspiration for Robinson Crusoe and also the model for the Spy-glass in Robert Louis Stevenson's Treasure Island. Tucked away in St Thomas Lane between nineteenth-century industrial premises was the Seven Stars, a notorious haunt of slave traders in the eighteenth century. There were many other public houses in the city centre which were in existence before 1800. In the nineteenth century the public house was an important place of working-class entertainment, and in districts such as Barton Hill, Easton and Bedminster there were many public houses built in the second half of the nineteenth century. The Llandoger Trow was one of just a handful of free houses in the city; the great majority were tied houses belonging to George's, Bristol's largest brewer, although Ushers and Simonds also owned pubs in the city. George's came to dominate brewing in Bristol in the late nineteenth century through a series of take-overs of competitors. Their expansion in the early twentieth century was also based on the sale of bottled beers, which were sold in the city's numerous off-licences. The firm's biggest rival, the Bristol United Brewery, was absorbed in 1956 and its brewery in Lewins Mead closed down; then in 1961 George's was taken over by Courage. Many public houses were lost in the blitz and many more were victims of post-war clearances when small street corner pubs and off-licences were swept away. Pubs were at first excluded from the pre-war council estates; residents of the new houses in Sea Mills, for example, had to walk to

Westbury-on-Trym or Shirehampton before finding a pub. Nevertheless, after the war public houses were established in areas of new housing. By 1969 the number of public houses in Bristol had increased to 430, although this was a lower density than fifty years earlier.

Market entrance from All Saints Lane, 1930s: an atmospheric scene as sunshine streams into this narrow passageway which runs from Corn Street to St Nicholas Street. The tower of St Nicholas' church is in the distance beyond the Crown public house. The Crown was one of the few free houses in the city and is advertising draught Bass. The Market was designed by Samuel Glascodine and opened in 1745 for the sale of meat and vegetables; it remained in use as a wholesale fruit market until 1968 when a new one in St Phillips was opened.

Withecombs, tobacconists, Bridge Street, *c.* 1936. A smartly dressed young woman wearing a fashionable stole around her neck buys a packet of twenty cigarettes – either Wills Gold Flake or Players Navy Cut – for 1*s* from a coin slot machine outside Withecombs shop in Bridge Street. Prominent in the window display is a commemorative shield marking the 1935 Jubilee of King George V. This was a boom time for the tobacco industry and retailers: between 1928 and 1940 *per capita* consumption of tobacco and cigarettes practically doubled.

Wilsons, ladies outfitters, Castle Street from Cock and Bottle Lane, late 1930s. In the heart of the pre-war shopping centre, Wilsons store, established in 1933, advertises new spring fashions; there is a hairdressing salon on the first floor and a restaurant and cafe on the lower ground floor. The main sign is in sans serif lettering, which became fashionable in the 1930s, and is illuminated by neon lights. Pre-war Castle Street contained several other clothes shops, including Stuckey's outfitters on the left-hand corner of Cock and Bottle Lane. Several major chain stores including Boots, British Home Stores, Burtons, Marks & Spencer and Woolworths were also located in Castle Street; and the Bristol Co-operative Society had its head offices there.

The Lower Arcade, Broadmead, *c.* 1950. A blind man passes the Broadmead entrance to the Lower Arcade, designed by James Foster and built in 1825. The arcade runs between the Horsefair and Broadmead and was threatened by the post-war plans for the new Broadmead shopping centre, but the planned demolition was reversed in 1947 following protests from the Council for the Protection of Ancient Bristol and others.

Broadmead, looking towards the Odeon and Nelson Street, late 1950s. The Dolcis shop has been claimed as the most imaginative modern shop in the new centre: the façade, according to John Punter, was 'a sophisticated play between transparent planes that was especially striking at night'. Before the war Dolcis had its shop was on the corner of Wine Street and Dolphin Street.

John Lewis's Store, the Horsefair, *c.* 1958. This department store of startling white Portland stone was built on the site of St James's churchyard and designed by Sir Percy Thomas. The store, the largest in Bristol, opened on 26 September 1958 and became an important part of the Broadmead shopping centre until April 1998, when the company relocated to the out-of-town shopping centre at Cribbs Causeway.

New shops on the corner of Broadmead and Union Street, September 1953. The premises of Swears and Wells, furriers, was designed by the City Architect in the restrained modern style that he was promoting for the whole of Broadmead. The Woolworths store was designed by the company's own architect, who adopted a more futuristic façade above set-back display windows, while H. Samuel, next door, chose a façade with recessed curtain walling within a Bath stone frame. Before the war, H. Samuel and Swears and Wells were located in Wine Street and Woolworths in Castle Street.

Park Street, *c.* 1935. Rising from College Green to Clifton, Park Street was one of the city's principal shopping streets with a reputation for high-quality shops. Barr's saddlers shop on the left was soon to be demolished to make way for the site of the new Council House on College Green.

Park Street, 1950s. Originally entitled 'Rainy Day Reflections', this photograph provides a surprising double image of the Wills building reflected in a shop window. Designed by Sir George Oatley, the Wills building was opened by King George V and Queen Mary on 9 June 1925.

Queens Road, *c.* 1930: a pre-war scene of this up-market shopping street. Maggs' sign partially covers the first-floor windows of the elegant Royal Parade built in the 1850s (see *Bristol 1850–1919*, page 71). Established in about 1857 as bedding manufacturers and house furnishers, Maggs & Co. opened its department store in the Royal Parade, Queens Road, in about 1895, selling a wide range of goods including furniture, electrical goods, ironmongery, gardening tools, china and glass. Duck Son & Pinker was started in Bath in 1848 and in Bristol in 1886. The Bristol branch was originally located at 13 Queens Road and subsequently at 1 Royal Parade, where they had extensive showrooms on three floors stocked with pianos, harmoniums and organs. The Queens Road premises were blitzed during the war. The building on the right is the headquarters of Lennards Ltd, boot and shoe makers; it was completely destroyed in the Blitz.

Interior view of the entrance hall of the headquarters of Lennards Ltd, 1923. Established in 1877, the company claimed to be one of the largest shoe businesses in the British Empire with over two hundred branches, fifteen of which were in Bristol. Shoes were sold worldwide by mail order from Bristol. With its corner clock tower, the building was a prominent landmark in Queen's Road until it was bombed in the war. The company had a shoe factory in Northampton and its own holiday and convalescent home for staff at Weston-super-Mare.

e showroom windows of Beacon House, Queens Road, shine brightly in the gathering dusk – signalling the new era of nestic electricity, *c.* 1933. Hitherto, Gardiner Sons & Co. Ltd, established in 1860, had concentrated largely on hitectural foundry work and wholesale ironmongery sold from their premises in Nelson Street, but the opening of se showrooms in 1933 represented a major shift towards retail trading. An advertisement in Kellys Directory for 1933 ited the customer to 'inspect these super showrooms' containing 'a splendid selection' of household ironmongery, den tools and ornaments, fireplaces and cooking stoves, bathroom fittings and the newest electrical goods'. The lding began life as the Queens Hotel in October 1854. Gardiner's sold Beacon House in 1957 when they moved to ad Plain, and the building was subsequently occupied by Taylors, Debenhams and Habitat.

The red telephone box was then a relatively new addition to the street scene. Designed by the architect Sir Giles bert Scott and first introduced in London in 1926, this type of kiosk with several variations became widely established Bristol and elsewhere during the 1930s. Tramlines in the road reflect the light of the electric street lamp, first roduced in the city in 1893.

Bristol Co-operative Society butcher's shop, 44 Chelsea Road, Easton, *c.* 1936. The Bristol Co-operative Society was founded in 1884 to give members a share in the profits on the sale of a wide range of goods and each member was paid a dividend based on the value of their purchases. The Society ran nineteen butchery branches in Bristol in the mid-1930s; a co-operative grocery store was located next door to this butcher's shop.

C. Allen & Co., motor agents, 159 Whiteladies Road, *c.* 1936. Smartly attired attendants in white overalls and peaked caps are photographed alongside Armstrong Siddeley saloon cars. C. Allen & Sons were established at these premises from about 1934 but had gone by 1947. The 1920s and 1930s saw a marked growth in retail outlets catering for the increasing numbers of motorists. Barclays Bank on the corner of Burlington Road is seen on the extreme left.

Aitken's shoe repair shop, 6 Abbotsford Road, Cotham, mid-1920s. This business was started in 1919 by Edward (Ted) Aitken who then opened a second shop in Sandy Park, Brislington, which continued until his death in 1941. The business was continued by his son, Ivor, in Cotham Hill until 1985. The shop window is crowded with advertisements for Cherry Blossom and Nugget shoe polish, and displays of inner soles, heels and other shoe accessories.

Connett's, drapers, 116 Whiteladies Road, 1920s. Ladies' underwear, lace and ties can be identified in the window display of this shop, which was established by William George Connett in about 1908. A second shop was opened at 408 Gloucester Road, Horfield, in about 1925. The Whiteladies Road shop was still in business in 1969.

Shops in Syme's Avenue, Hartcliffe, late 1950s. Bristol's post-war council estates acquired their own local shopping centres, with shops similar in design to these in Hartcliffe. The ice cream van belongs to Verrechia, who started selling ice cream in Bristol in 1925 and is credited with introducing the ice cream van to Britain.

Grocer's shop, *c.* 1947. The customer is ready with her book of coupons. Rationing had been introduced during the war and remained in force until 1954. There was a worsening for the domestic consumer after 1945: bread, which had not been rationed at any time during the war, was rationed between July 1946 and July 1947 and potatoes at the end of 1947.

G. Thorne, grocer and tobacconist, on the corner of Muller Road and Stapleton Road, Eastville, 1960s. Brook Bond, TyPhoo and Lyons Tea are advertised in the window along with Wall's ice cream, Heinz baked beans and Birds Eye foods. The thirteen-arch railway viaduct in the background carried the line of the former Midland Railway to Avonmouth, and was demolished in 1968 to make way for the construction of the M32 motorway.

Park Side filling and service station, Stapleton Road, Eastville, mid-1960s. Two female petrol attendants in overalls chat in the doorway of the shop between serving Cleveland petrol (a subsidiary of Esso) to motorists at prices ranging from 5*s* 2½*d* to 5*s* 9*d* a gallon. For 2*d* extra the customer received a double strip of 'pink stamps'; these, like the rival 'Green Shield' stamps, were collected in books which could be exchanged for gifts. From the 1970s many small petrol stations such as this fell before competition from larger 'self-service' garages owned by the petrol companies.

The Llandoger Trow, King Street, 1930s. Occupying the right-hand house of a group of five gabled timber-framed houses built in 1664, the Llandoger Trow can be traced to 1775; the name refers to the flat-bottomed trows or boats built at Llandogo on the Wye that sailed across the Bristol Channel to Welsh Back. The two end houses were destroyed in the blitz and the pub now occupies all three surviving houses, but in this pre-war view the next house is occupied by F.C. Brummel, plumber and electrician. In the 1920s he is listed in trade directories as a plumber and gas fitter, but, moving with the times, was advertising his services as an electrician by the 1930s.

The Railway Inn, Stapleton Road, 1930s. Stapleton Road railway station opened in 1863 and the public house first appears in local trade directories for 1867; in the 1930s it was one of over 900 licensed premises in Bristol and the surrounding area belonging to George's Brewery. There are thirteen identical buff earthenware chimney pots on the two stacks.

The Royal Hotel on the corner of Gloucester Road and Clayton Street, Avonmouth, 1930s. This attractive row of late nineteenth-century shops including the hotel was built in the Domestic Revival Style with attractive gables and moulded brick chimneys; the steps surrounding the block were apparently intended as a flood barrier.

The Rising Sun, corner of Lower Castle Street and Ellbroad Street, *c.* 1950. This public house is listed in Mathew's Bristol Directory for 1794; having been rebuilt around the turn of the century it was demolished in 1954.

CHAPTER FIVE

HOUSING & DOMESTIC LIFE

In 1920 most people in Bristol lived in privately owned rented accommodation. Home ownership was rare, and although Bristol's first council houses had been built in Chapel Street and Mina Road in about 1901, working-class people lived mostly in Victorian terraced houses located in the industrial suburbs or occupied rooms in tenements, many of slum standard, close to the city centre. Houses were gas lit; cooking still commonly took place on coal burning kitchen ranges – although the use of gas cookers was rapidly increasing; and a brick and iron wash-copper was used for the weekly wash: this task, traditionally allotted to Mondays, was hard, labour-intensive work. The majority of smaller homes had no bathroom or inside toilet. Middle-class homes were larger and better equipped, but their occupants were having to adjust to a shortage of servants following the end of the First World War. Early issues of *Homes and Gardens*, first published in 1919 and catering for a middle-class audience, featured labour-saving domestic arrangements for the 'servantless house'. Over the next fifty years the way people lived in Bristol changed radically as a revolution occurred in the quality of housing and living standards.

A fundamental shift in attitude towards the provision of working-class housing occurred towards the end of the First World War. By 1918 there was, nationwide, an acute shortage of housing: it was clear that private developers would not be able to supply houses in the quantity – and of the quality expected – at rents that the average working-class family could afford. So the government intervened, and in 1919 the Liberal Minister of Health, Sir Christopher Addison, introduced a Housing Act which required local authorities to survey their housing needs and make good the deficiency with the assistance of a generous government subsidy. Anticipating the legislation, Bristol City Council established a Housing Extensions & Town Planning Committee in March 1918 and quickly formed a plan of action. Village suburbs were to be created across the city, and before the end of the year land was purchased in Sea Mills, Shirehampton and Knowle. In 1919 Bristol's first council house built under the terms of the Addison Act was completed in Beechen Drive, Fishponds.

A total of 1,189 Addison houses were built in Bristol. In 1919, however, the housing shortage in Bristol was reckoned to stand at 5,000 dwellings, so this first wave of council building fell short of meeting the city's housing needs. Nevertheless, the new estates in Fishponds, Sea Mills and Bedminster represented a complete break with the past and expressed a totally new approach to working-class housing. Local authority control of the Victorian working-class suburb was largely restricted to ensuring that new houses were sanitary, but little else. They were not planned but grew piecemeal, according to the vagaries of speculative development by small builders and other entrepreneurs. The new council estates were, in complete contrast, planned environments, designed and controlled by the Council; this was not simply a policy of rehousing, it was also institutionalised social engineering creating a new pattern of life for thousands of people. The estates were conceived as self-contained communities with churches, schools and shops, although public houses were at first excluded. Their layout followed the guidelines set by the Tudor Walters report published in 1918, which drew heavily on the garden city ideal introduced at the end of the nineteenth century. The Tudor Walters Committee criticised the typical late nineteenth-century working-class suburb for the monotony of the long, parallel rows of houses, and the houses themselves – for their narrow frontages and rear projections which obstructed light and air at the back. Instead, the new council developments aimed to create self-sufficient cottage homes in low-density garden suburbs, and following the recommendations of the Tudor Walters Report there were to be no more than twelve houses to an acre. The first estates in Fishponds and Sea Mills incorporated a mixture of different house types; rows of four were combined with semi-detached houses, designed in a simple cottage style and employing traditional building materials. The interior plan of the houses also varied: the basic distinction was between houses with a parlour and those without; all houses, however, had a scullery and all were equipped with a bath. The houses were given generous sized plots with gardens front and back. While providing a relaxed setting, the idea was also to encourage the tenants to grow vegetables. Some of the houses were laid out in attractive crescents – as at Sea Mills, Fishponds and Knowle Park – avoiding the monotony associated with the long straight rows of Victorian terraces. In Knowle, Broad Walk – laid out from the mid-1920s – was designed as a wide, tree-lined boulevard: the contrast with the older inner city suburbs could not have been greater.

In 1923 Neville Chamberlain, Minister of Health in the new Conservative government, passed another Housing Act which aimed to encourage building by private enterprise. This Act constituted a complete reversal of the 1919 policy of encouraging local authorities to become major providers of working-class housing. Only 1,655 council houses were built in Bristol under this scheme, although the subsidy did stimulate private house building. Another change in government – this time the first Labour administration – resulted in yet another Housing Act, introduced by J. Wheatley, the new Minister of Health, which restored the local authority subsidy for house building. It remained in operation until 1933 and is generally regarded as the most successful of the inter-war housing measures. In Bristol 7,114 houses were financed under the Wheatley subsidy; they were generally smaller than the earlier houses, elevations were simpler and there were more short terraces in place of crescents, as building in straight rows was less expensive. Non-traditional building methods were tried, including metal frame construction – such as the 'Dorman Long'-type houses built in Sylvan Way, Sea Mills, in 1926. Experiments were also made with concrete houses, and in Knowle Park with all-metal houses, which suffered from condensation.

The new council estates, however, did not supply the needs of the poorer sections of the working class. Rents remained high and sub-letting was forbidden upon pain of eviction. As a result, only the higher paid worker could afford them, leaving the mass of poorer workers living in older properties – some of them slums and many located near the centre. By the late 1920s attention was turning to their plight, and in 1930 a new Housing Act was passed which introduced a subsidy for the clearance of slums and the re-housing of the families displaced. The scheme was delayed by the economic crisis of 1931 but in 1933, following the passing of another Housing Act, Bristol City Council approved a programme for the clearance of 2,900 slum properties. These were located chiefly in parts of Bedminster, St Phillips, St Judes and other inner city areas; following demolition, the occupants were rehoused in new council houses erected in Bedminster and Knowle.

By 1939 the occupants of 3,500 slum clearance houses had been rehoused. Economies in standards continued: there were more of the cheaper non-parlour houses, for example, and the estates containing the rehoused slum families, as in Knowle West, came to be seen in the popular mind as 'rough', as opposed to the older estates such as Sea Mills, which were perceived as 'respectable'. Nevertheless, the former slum dwellers were probably unaware of such fine distinctions: what mattered to them was the huge improvement in their environment: compare the scene in Weare's Buildings illustrated on page 99 with the spacious setting of the houses in Wordsworth Road in Horfield on page 108. One former occupant of a slum recalls her excitement as a young child of seven moving to a new council house in Knowle West in 1935. Her family had occupied two rooms at the top of a four-storey tenement in Houlton Street, St Judes, where there was one toilet in the back yard for all the residents. The move represented an almost imaginable improvement in living standards. They now had an entire house to themselves. The house was still lit by gas but it had a bathroom, whereas in St Judes they had used a galvanised zinc bath, hung on a nail in the yard, which was carried inside and used in front of the fire. The kitchen was provided with a gas boiler which made the task of the weekly wash a lot easier. They had a garden – space for children to play in – and there was plenty of greenery and trees; compared with St Judes, Knowle West was like the countryside. The division between work and home which had characterised the Victorian and Edwardian middle-class suburbs was now extended to the working-class suburb. Living on a new council estate on the edge of the city left many residents with a considerably longer journey to work, and the benefits of the new, well-equipped home had to be weighed against the sense of isolation which some residents clearly felt. Life on the new estates could be dull. The provision of amenities such as shops and leisure facilities often lagged far behind the building of the homes: there were no shops in Sea Mills, for example, until 1929.

Between 1919 and 1939 some 36,000 houses were built in Bristol: 14,500 of these were council houses but about 60 per cent were built by private builders responding to the demand from middle-class house buyers, the 'owner-earners' as one 1930s Bristol builder called them. The middle class expanded markedly after 1920, particularly because of the increase in non-manual occupations in management, teaching, administrative and clerical work. The new recruits were keen to demonstrate their arrival by assuming a lifestyle which separated them from the respectable working-class origins from which they had, in many cases, risen. Their predominant aspiration was to own a house, and in the 1920s and 1930s low interest rates coupled with the easier availability of mortgages, rising real wages, and falling building costs after 1930, brought home ownership within the reach of many for the first time. Home ownership was encouraged by the expansion of building societies, such as the Bristol & West, who supplied affordable mortgages, while the access to the house market was provided by an ever increasing number of estate agents.

Middle-class suburban development represented, above all, by the pebble-dashed, three bedroom 'semi', was widespread across Bristol but particularly extensive in the north-west of the city, which, based on Victorian and Edwardian building in Sneyd Park, Redland and Henleaze, was already established as a desirable area. The estates built in the 1920s and 1930s continued the outward movement towards the edge of the city where residents could create a respectable and secure environment free of the undesirable associations of city life. They consisted mostly of speculative ventures by builders who bought land from country landowners: the Harfords, for example, owners of the Blaise Castle Estate, Henbury, until 1926, sold land in Westbury-on-Trym for residential development between the wars; Falcondale Road, a mid-1930s development, was named after their residence near Lampeter in Wales. The builders aimed to provide low-density houses (usually no more than twelve per acre) in a variety of house styles – providing an element of individuality and a range of prices. Thus Kellaway Avenue, Horfield, laid out in 1920, was subsequently filled with a mixed development of houses and bungalows. The latter became popular in the 1920s, offering small yet detached accommodation, ideal for older people.

Three estates in Stapleton, Stoke Bishop and Westbury-on-Trym, developed simultaneously by Stone & Co., Redland-based builders, in the mid-1930s when the building boom was at its height, illustrate the range of houses available. The cheapest were located on the Colston Estate in Stapleton overlooking Eastville Park, where three types of relatively plain semi-detached three bedroomed houses were available in 1936 from £565. Semis were also built on the Druid Stoke and Henbury Hill Estates, although several

Dowry Square, May 1956. The City Council's 1952 Development Report calculated that there were 35,000 houses predating 1880 in the city, those in Dowry Square being some of the earliest. The houses in the square were built between 1720 and about 1750 to provide fashionable lodgings for visitors to the nearby Hotwells.

different designs of detached houses ranging in price from £975 to £1,500 were included. All the houses on the three estates were designed by Bristol architects, including Alec French and James & Meredith. Architectural embellishments increased with the price of the house. The façades of the Colston Estate were similar to council houses – apart from their two-storey bay window – but the more expensive designs on the other two estates contained a rich mixture of traditional motifs which characterised this house type all over Britain. Tile-hung walls, leaded casement windows and mock half-timbered gables drew on traditional vernacular – or cottage-style – architecture. The steeply pitched roof of the house in Falcondale Road illustrated on page 111 recalls the picturesque, fantasy designs of Blaise Hamlet by John Nash (1752–1835) less than 2 miles away. Gothic motifs such as embattled walls added to the variety and catered for the owner's wish for a home with individual character. Yet no amount of dressing up in retrospective styles could hide the essential 1930s character of these houses, with their often harsh red brickwork and grey pebble-dash. The building of a few houses in the modernistic International Style in Stoke Bishop at least introduced a note of originality of design, but their stark white walls, flat roofs and curved glass bay windows never won popular appeal.

The interior layout of the typical 1930s private house combined traditional values with modern requirements. The Victorian convention of segregated room use was maintained with the two principal ground-floor rooms serving as lounge and dining room. Separate access to these was provided from the hall, which, frequently panelled in oak, complemented the traditional house exterior and provided an appropriate backdrop to a display of antique or reproduction furniture, copper and brassware. Stairways were often traditional with turned balusters, but simpler designs which required less dusting became popular in the 1930s. Convenience within the home was important to this servantless middle class, larger than its Edwardian predecessor but also poorer, and labour-saving arrangements – especially in the kitchen – became an important consideration in their design. By the 1920s cooking over a coal-burning kitchen range was rapidly giving way to cooking by gas, which was cleaner and easier to use. In 1935 the Bristol Gas Company claimed to have 105,000 gas cookers in use in the city (in about 90 per cent of homes), and these were available either through hire purchase or cheap weekly rents. Gas boilers for doing the weekly wash were also widely adopted, replacing the coal-fired wash copper as seen in the scullery on page 107. However, by the early 1930s gas was facing stiff competition from electricity. Between the mid-1920s and the early 1930s electricity was laid in most streets in the city, and in 1929 a new large power station built by the City Council's Electric Department at Portishead was brought into use. The increase in the domestic consumption of electricity in Bristol was dramatic: in 1924 there were 14,397 users; by 1935 the figure had increased to 71,935 (over 63 per cent of all households). In 1929 a Bristol branch of the Electrical Association for Women was established, and in 1934 built an all-electric house in Stoke Bishop – in the modern style, appropriately – to demonstrate the potential of electricity in the home, its convenience and cleanliness. Notwithstanding the interest, locally and nationally, in this demonstration, the impact of electrical appliances was uneven: electric irons were readily adopted and vacuum cleaners were also popular, but the widespread use of electric cookers and washing machines had to wait until the 1950s.

House building came to a virtual standstill during the war, and the pre-war housing shortage was exacerbated by the destruction of 3,000 homes by enemy action. Temporary accommodation was provided by pre-fabricated houses; over 3,000 were erected in Ashton Vale, Sea Mills, Westbury-on Trym and elsewhere. While these proved popular with their occupants they were only ever intended as a temporary measure and the provision of new council housing was the City's top priority after 1945. Building soon resumed in the same spirit of optimism which surrounded official plans for the remodelling of the city centre. The break in the house building programme caused by the war gave planners the opportunity to review housing policy; they were guided by the findings of the Dudley Commission published in 1944, which like the earlier Tudor Walters Report reviewed existing housing types and made recommendations for future house building. The report was critical of the monotony of the typical pre-war council estate and recommended that a greater variety of house types was introduced. This criticism was held widely. The repetition of the same or very similar architectural units had created a dull, repetitive urban landscape, which, moreover, consisted of a single class. Achieving greater physical diversity in house types and mixing social groups were seen as vital to future developments, and these principles were embodied in the notion of the 'neighbourhood unit', which became a widely held planning concept after the war.

Neighbourhood units were perceived as self-contained communities including a wide mix of house types – and therefore social groups – supported by schools, libraries, health and recreational facilities and factories to provide local employment. In its first Development Plan published in 1952, the City Council asserted that sub-division of Bristol into neighbourhood units would foster 'a co-operative spirit between the social classes . . . to overcome the social and civic difficulties from which the large city suffers'. Adoption of the neighbourhood unit, therefore, represented more than a housing policy: the City was assuming responsibility for social planning – and while this had been a feature of council estate design ever since the idea of village suburbs was first mooted in 1918, post-war policy represented a far greater level of control over all Bristolians and their homes than had ever previously existed.

The neighbourhood unit principle was applied to all the new post-war housing estates at Henbury, Lawrence Weston, Lockleaze, Stockwood and Hartcliffe, and also to the redevelopment of older areas such as Barton Hill. A greater mix of house types characterised these areas, and included blocks and flats as well as prefabricated houses of steel and concrete, such as the 'Woolaway' houses built in Lawrence Weston and

Henbury in the early 1950s. A small number of flats had been built by the Council before the war in Hotwells, but the fashion for high-rise flats originated in the 1920s and 1930s among architects of the Modern Movement. One of the earliest post-war blocks in Bristol was St Peter's House, an eight-storey block of maisonettes on the corner of Hotwell and Jacobs Wells Road, which curiously combined traditional services behind a modern façade: each maisonette was heated by a coal fire fitted with a back boiler supplying heat to radiators in the two bedrooms. Each dwelling had a coal bunker off the kitchen, while massive chimney flues ran through the centre of the two main wings. Later blocks, built after the 1956 Clean Air Act, were designed with full central heating.

At Barton Hill the creation of a neighbourhood unit involved the construction of high-rise blocks from the mid-1950s while retaining some of the streets of Victorian terraced houses. The intention was to retain a sense of community, which clearly did not flourish within a tower block. The flats were ugly and jarring on the outside, and their occupants often felt a sense of isolation; without gardens, the flats were unsuitable for families with children. Nevertheless, blocks of flats continued to be built into the mid-1960s – at Redcliff, Lawrence Weston, Hartcliffe and Kingsdown – but mounting criticism of their social (and visual) shortcomings and the structural failure of the Ronan Point block in London in 1968 caused a strong reaction against further building of this type of accommodation. In practice, the idea of the neighbourhood unit fell far short of its original objectives. Arguably, the greatest success was achieved in Henbury where the visual and social impact of the Council-built houses and flats in the 1950s was diluted by the existence of an historic village centre, and where extensive private house building occurred in the 1960s. Lawrence Weston, Lockleaze and particularly Hartcliffe failed, however, to achieve the diverse social mix originally projected, and ironically these estates came to be particularly associated with those social problems that the neighbourhood unit was intended to solve. Their isolation – social and geographical – has, nevertheless, created over time a strong sense of community on these estates, notwithstanding the very real social problems which exist.

By the end of 1972, 33,461 council homes had been built – twice the number built before the war – housing about 40 per cent of Bristol's population. Home ownership continued to increase, reflecting improved standards of living, and many new private homes were built in the late 1950s and 1960s. Across Bristol, from Stockwood to Henbury, housing developments by large national companies, such as Wimpey, took place. Exterior design easily distinguished them from council property: white painted weatherboarding or cedarwood cladding in imitation of Scandinavian style were popular – so, too, were dormer windows – and owing to the widespread adoption of central heating, chimneys all but disappeared. Acknowledging the rapid increase in car ownership, most had a garage. Privately built post-war houses were often smaller than their pre-war counterparts, but in responding to increased informality in family life the open-plan interior was widely adopted. Generally, in terms of space and amenity standards, the gap between the 'middle class' and 'working-class' home, which had been particularly marked in the early twentieth century, had considerably narrowed. Most people had benefited from the huge improvements, therefore, which occurred between the 1920s and 1960s.

Weare's Buildings, Bedminster, 17 November 1931. The photograph provides a fascinating record of a 1930s slum: many of the residents have come outside their front doors to be in the photograph taken by the City Council shortly before demolition; women and children predominate – the men being at work, or just out. With Hope Square, which ran close to the back of the row on the left, these Georgian houses of about 1810 to 1820 formed a small self-contained world, hemmed in by adjoining factories and reached only by a narrow passage-way from York Road, off to the right. By 1930 they ranked among the worst slum properties in the city, and were condemned in 1931 in accordance with the 1930 Housing Act; the inhabitants were rehoused in new council houses in Bedminster and Knowle.

They were two-up, two-down dwellings: two bedrooms were reached by a narrow twisting stairway located between the front parlour and the kitchen. The kitchens had a range with an oven and opened on to a tiny back yard – 9 ft by 5 ft – which contained a sink and cold water tap open to the elements. On one side of the yard, housed in a small, single-storey lean-to, was a WC without a flush, and on the other side was another small structure housing a washing copper. The yards and outhouses of Hope Square backed on to those of Weare's Buildings, so that the rear walls of the two rows of houses were only about 10 ft apart, providing little light and poor ventilation. While there were narrow gardens at the front with valuable space for drying washing, they, too, must have seen little sun and appear to contain old junk and wooden hutches. Added to the almost perpetual gloom in which the occupants lived, they also had to tolerate the smells at close quarters from two of the most obnoxious industries conceivable – leather tanning and the manufacture of glue from animal bones. No wonder the incidence of mortality and disease was high in this little quarter.

Dereliction and squalor at the rear of eighteenth-century houses, May 1956. The first three houses on the left face on to Hope Square – see opposite top – while the front of the two houses on the right of the picture are on Granby Hill. All these houses survive.

Hope Square, May 1956. The late eighteenth-century houses overlooking the square, seen here, joined the row of houses on Granby Hill at an acute angle (i.e. less than ninety degrees) with the result that the windows of the two houses in the corner, just visible on the extreme left, look into each other. The houses on the square were subsequently refurbished, but most of those on the Granby Hill side were replaced with private flats.

'Bin day' in Langton Street, Cathay, *c.* 1950. This attractive view of Langton Street, looking towards St Mary Redcliffe, shows one of several streets of small, late-Georgian terraces developed along the north bank of the New Cut following completion of the Floating Harbour in 1809. In the late 1950s and early 1960s they were cleared to make way for several large blocks of council flats.

Greenbank Avenue, Lower Easton, mid-1950s. These terraced houses built in about 1898 have a single-storey bay window which shares a roof with the neighbouring bay. The narrow frontages of small Victorian terraces like this were criticised in the 1919 Tudor Walters Report, which set the standards for subsequent council house design and much suburban development – private and public alike – over the next few decades, aiming to provide a more spacious environment in place of the congestion and monotony of older developments like this.

The rear view of the houses seen from the front, above, in Greenbank Avenue, mid-1950s. Rear extensions containing a back kitchen were a feature of most working-class terraced houses built in the second half of the nineteenth century; Many consisted of two storeys – the upper room serving as a small third bedroom – but this row has only single-storey extensions containing a scullery nearest the house; next is the WC with its unmistakable saw-tooth door (providing ventilation),and the coal shed at the back.

Hallway of 65 Elmdale Road, Bedminster, September 1956. Built in 1901, this house has a narrow hall with an inner front door embellished with ruby, blue and etched glass and a decorative arch supporting the bedroom wall above. The stairs are on the right beyond the door to the front parlour while the back room – sometimes called the kitchen – contains a fitted dresser. The back kitchen still has the original kitchen range but these had generally fallen out of use in Bristol by the 1930s with the adoption of gas cookers, one of which can be clearly seen on the left.

Glendare Street, Barton Hill before redevelopment, 11 November 1953. Barton Hill grew after the opening of the Feeder Canal and the Great Western Cotton Factory in 1838. By 1952 it was one of the most densely populated areas in the city – consisting mainly of nineteenth-century terraced houses with negligible public or private open space. The houses on the left were demolished to make way for Glendare House, an eleven-storey block of flats constructed in 1958 and demolished in 1995 because of problems with its construction. The low hill beyond the end of the street was the 'Brillos', a chemical waste tip.

Backs of old houses in Cathay, Redcliff, *c.* 1950. These houses were demolished shortly afterwards to make way for a council development of blocks of flats built in the 1950s. The cutting in the foreground is the Bristol Harbour line from Temple Meads to the docks, which passed into a tunnel beneath Pump Lane. The railway line closed in 1964 but the embankment remains, and Pump Lane, immediately east of St Mary Redcliffe, retains its granite sets. The steep slope of Totterdown is visible to the left of St Luke's church, while the white smoke below the hill probably belongs to a steam train on its way to the south-west.

King Street looking across Whitehouse Street to Hillgrove Street, Bedminster, *c.* 1950. Before the war the area between York Road and the main railway line to the south-west was a densely packed area of streets of small terraced houses and shops. There were three public houses alone on Whitehouse Street: the Masons Arms, the Angel and the Barley Mow. Several bombs fell here during the blitz, including a land mine which completely destroyed the Chequers public house; the Masons Arms was also destroyed in a bomb raid. Cleared after the war, the area became the site of the Bedminster Trading Estate, with the first factories in business by 1952.

The view across King Street to Parker Brothers Tannery in Whitehouse Street, Bedminster, *c.* 1950. The Angel public house opposite the tannery on the corner of Sargent Street had closed by the mid-1950s.

Old Quarry Road, Penpole Housing Estate, 1950s. The 150 dwellings on this estate were built by the Ministry of Munitions towards the end of the First World War to house munitions workers, and were purchased soon afterwards by the City Council. Consisting mainly of blocks of four and six, with generous sized gardens, the houses were arranged on three new roads near Avonmouth: Kings Weston Avenue, Old Quarry Road and The Bean Acre.

The living room of a house in Old Quarry Road, 1950s. While the external design and layout of the council estates after 1919 represented a complete break with the past, the internal arrangements relied upon proven Victorian technology: gas lighting and coal-fired cooking; the joinery details, including the fitted dresser beside the range and the picture rail, are also traditional in design. The room preserves something of the flavour of a Victorian parlour in this 1950s view, even though it has acquired electric lighting and a radio.

Scullery, Old Quarry Road, 1950s. This scene, reminiscent of a seventeenth-century Dutch painting, shows the basic facilities of a 1920s council house scullery: a single cold tap over a white ceramic sink, a wooden drain board and, on the right, a coal-fired washing copper used to boil clothes and usually lit early on Monday mornings. The staggered brickwork of the flue from the copper can be seen against the wall. Tide washing powder was introduced by Proctor & Gamble in 1950.

Melton Crescent, Horfield, *c.* 1930. A turning off Wordsworth Road developed between 1926 and 1929, Melton Crescent contains a mixture of house types including semi-detached houses with and without gables, and blocks of four houses. Wordsworth Road runs across the picture, while the unfinished road in the foreground is Bonnington Walk. The mix of house types created a more spacious and carefully planned environment than the rows of Victorian terraces, but the scheme was repeated with little variation over too large an area: each turning off Wordsworth Road was treated the same way, with a semi-detached gabled house placed on the corner at an angle. Unfortunately, the repetition created its own monotony, which was precisely the criticism levelled at council estates like this after the war.

Duckmore Road, Ashton, 11 July 1968. The Duckmore Road estate was developed by the Council in 1926. This photograph was taken after the heavy rainfall on the night of Wednesday 10 July 1968 when more than 4 in of rain fell on almost the whole of Bristol, flooding much of Ashton and Bedminster. Water rose to bedroom level at Brixham Road, Clinton Road and Marksbury Road, while Winterstoke Road was blocked for a quarter of a mile by water.

The Prince of Wales visiting new houses in Dings Walk, 6 November 1934. The Prince of Wales was particularly concerned with the problems of slum dwellers nationwide, and came to see these new homes built to replace nearby slums. The Royal Daimler carries the standard of the Prince of Wales.

No. 118 Fishponds Road, Eastville, 1956. The Lord Mayor and Lady Mayoress, Mr and Mrs Chamberlain, attract a crowd of curious onlookers as they inspect a Bristol Corporation housing improvement demonstration. Home improvement grants were made available for modernising older property to bring them up to accepted standards. This particular property had been purchased by the Council in 1956.

New private houses in Forest Road, Fishponds, *c.* 1925. About 60 per cent of the houses built in Bristol between the war were built by private developers.

The Bow dining set from the catalogue of Lenthall Brothers, furniture makers and upholsterers, Bedminster, *c.* 1935. Lenthall's produced a range of bedroom, dining room and living room suites in traditional style – evoking the Tudor period to complement the retrospective designs of the typical 1930s private house – or in the modern style. The Bow dining set, which was priced at 15 gns, curiously combines the two: the sideboard is in the modern style with rounded ends, while the dining table and chairs borrow motifs from the sixteenth and seventeenth century. Lenthalls named most of their range after local places: the catalogue includes Redcliffe, Backwell and Barton dining room suites, a Clevedon settee and easy chairs, and Wrington and Ashton bedroom suites.

A four-bedroom detached residence in Falcondale Road, designed by James and Meredith and illustrated in the 1936 brochure of Stone & Co., builders of Redland, Bristol. Falcondale Road was developed as part of the Henbury Hill Estate in the mid-1930s by Stone & Co., whose slogan was 'Architectural details faithfully interpreted'. The estate included houses ranging from semi-detached dwellings in Westover Close costing £750 to large detached houses built to 'suit purchasers' requirements' in Northover Road overlooking Henbury Golf Course: these started at £1,500. Double-fronted detached houses costing £995 were built on Passage Road, while slightly smaller houses in Falcondale Road were £975. The exterior design was a mixture of traditional motifs: the steeply pitched roof, tall chimney-stacks, leaded lights and hanging tiles in the double-storey bay window. Inside the emphasis was placed on convenience for the housewife, with an 'easiwork' kitchen and stairs built in the 'modern dust proof style'.

The 'Ashton' tiled fireplace, from the catalogue of the Metal Agencies Company, Winterstoke Road, 1954. This lounge fireplace with mottled eggshell tiles was typical of the 1930s to 1950s. With unconscious irony the MAC – celebrating their centenary year in 1954 – described this as a modern design with a semi-Tudor arch! In the 1960s tiled fireplaces rapidly fell from favour and rough stonework – or 'Cotswold stone' – fireplaces became popular; however, many new houses built after about 1960 were equipped with full central heating and had no fireplace: the centuries-old association between hearth and home had been broken.

Mother with twin pram, *c.* 1947. The photographs on these two pages are believed to have been taken by the Fry's official photographer for the City Council, probably for publicity purposes, to show the 'brave new world' of life on a city council estate in the immediate post-war years. The identity of the family and the precise location are unknown, but the setting may be Lawrence Weston, Henbury, or Southmead, where the building of council homes was proceeding at a dramatic rate at this time.

The fireplace forms the focal point of this council house living room and reading is the main recreation in about 1947, just a few years before the universal spread of television and the decline of open fires following the Clean Air Act of 1956. The furnishings appear fairly spartan, perhaps because the family have just moved in; father sits in a Lloyd Loom chair.

Chat over the garden fence, *c.* 1947. Council houses were generally provided with good sized gardens and the Council were keen that tenants should take up gardening and grow vegetables. The straight concrete path running down the centre was a common feature of the council house back garden and conveniently followed the route of the washing line.

A happy scene at tea-time: mother cuts the loaf of bread, which may have been rationed at the time, while father pours the tea. The wireless set presides over the scene. By 1947 BBC radio entertainment consisted of the Home Service, the Light Programme, a combination of light music, comedy and light drama, introduced in 1945 and the Third Programme, which followed in 1946. They provided the core of the BBC's radio network until 1967.

Aerial view of Lawrence Weston, looking south over the junction of Long Cross and Kings Weston Road, 195(Consisting of over 600 acres of farmland, this was one of several new housing estates developed shortly after the war, a within a decade had been transformed by the building of several thousand houses and blocks of flats. Shops, schoo churches and a library were provided to create a self-contained community, following the neighbourhood unit princi adopted by the City Council after the war. The City Council's 1952 Development Plan envisaged a population density nineteen people per acre in Lawrence Weston – less than half the average of Bristol's older industrial suburbs.

Hungerford Road, Stockwood Estate, late 1950s. 'Easyform' two-storey flats of concrete, cast on site, were built in 19 on the Stockwood Estate, 824 acres of agricultural land developed from the mid-1950s to rehouse people fr condemned property in the old inner city suburbs such as St Philip's Marsh.

A woman with her daughter receiving attention from a housing officer, possibly applying for council accommodation, *c.* 1948. In 1946 the waiting list for council housing reached a peak of 26,661, and dealing with this and other aspects of the management of the council estates led to the growth after 1919 of a large administrative workforce to meet the needs of tenants and, of course, to collect their rent.

Fifteen-storey blocks in Barton Hill, late 1950s. New blocks of flats were built in Barton Hill from the mid-1950s, starting with the fifteen-storey block Barton House. The City retained some of the older properties in this 22-acre 'neighbourhood unit' in order to prevent the old community from breaking up. Visually the result was disastrous, because of the difference in scale between the old and the new housing and the arid open spaces around the tower blocks.

St Peter's House, Jacob's Wells Road, late 1950s. The windowless side wall of this block of eight-storey maisonettes, designed by the City Architect, J. Nelson Meredith, in 1952, provides a backdrop to the belisha beacon on the pedestrian crossing at the bottom of Jacob's Wells Road. The block took its name from the late nineteenth-century church which stood on this site until 1939. The entrance to White Hart Steps leading up into Clifton was incorporated in the building, and can be seen on the left.

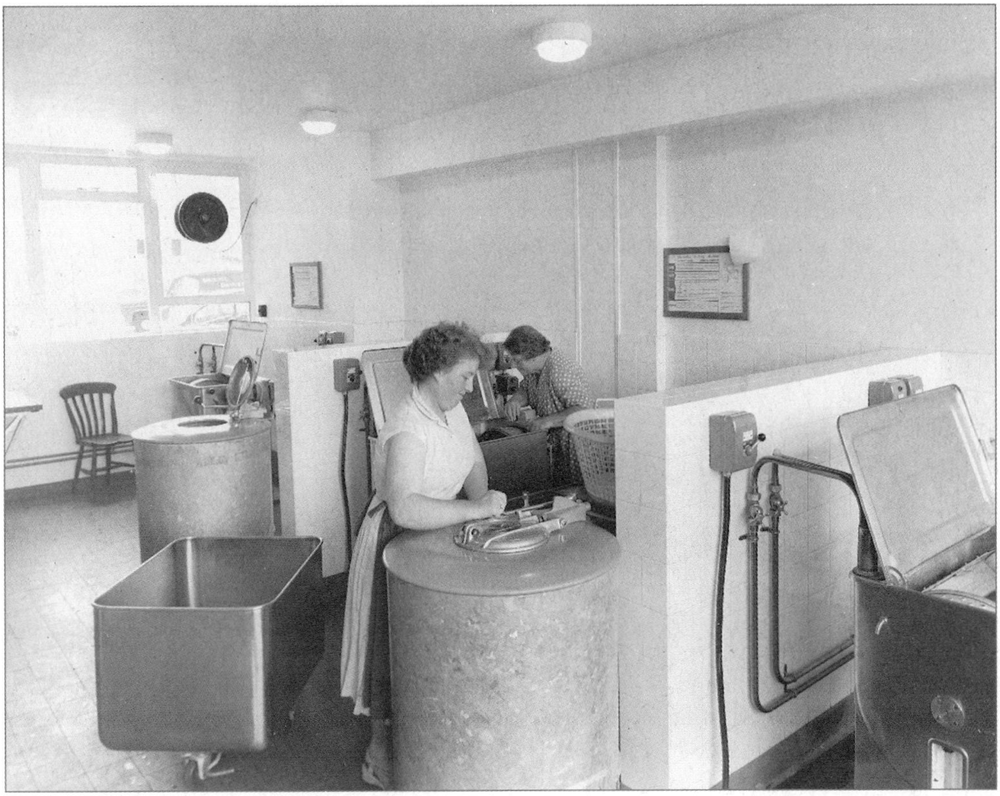

Laundry room in a council block, Redcliff, 22 July 1960. The council's post-war blocks of flats and maisonettes included a communal laundry, and this view shows the equipment that was standard for more than two decades: Electrolux washing machines with horizontal cylindrical tubs and large spin dryers. For the majority of residents who would have previously washed clothes using a gas or coal boiler followed by hand scrubbing, this was almost certainly their first encounter with an electric washing machine.

Waring House, Commercial Road, Redcliff, *c.* 1960. This huge L-shaped block of council maisonettes, flats and bedsits overlooking the New Cut was completed in 1960.

Norton Farmhouse, Station Road, Henbury, 1964. Many old farms lying on the outskirts of Bristol disappeared under bricks and mortar as Bristol continued its inexorable growth outwards. Norton Farm disappeared under private housing in 1964 and the old farmhouse with its large old-fashioned kitchen, dairy and cider cellar was demolished in August 1964.

Passage Road, Brentry, 1969. Passage Road contains Bristol's first pelican crossing, which opened in July 1969.

CHAPTER SIX

LEISURE & RECREATION

From the 1920s and 1930s leisure began to feature as prominently as work in the lives of Bristolians. People had more leisure time as average working hours fell from fifty-three hours a week at the beginning of the twentieth century to forty-two by the 1960s. During the 1920s one-and-a-half million wage earners were entitled to a holiday with pay; by 1938 the figure was three million; and as a result of the Holidays with Pay Act passed in that year the figure rose to eleven million. People also had more disposable income to spend on leisure pursuits: between 1913 and 1938 real wages increased by 50 per cent, while expenditure on such basics as food and rent decreased. Leisure time could be spent in a variety of ways. It was a matter of personal taste and of social class: going to the pub or a football match were predominantly working-class pursuits, while cricket and theatre-going tended to attract a middle-class audience. Many people looked to the theatre or cinema for entertainment, while others developed their leisure time in home-based activities such as gardening and other hobbies. Forms of entertainment tended to lose their local character: as cinema-goers watched American films in picture houses run by national companies, and at home families tuned in to the British Broadcasting Corporation from London, it became increasingly difficult to find a local identity to entertainment and leisure in Bristol.

In the 1920s and 1930s concerts, serious plays, pantomime and popular variety entertainment were staged at several theatres in Bristol. Classical concerts were held at the Colston Hall and the Victoria Assembly Rooms. The Prince's Theatre was visited by important touring companies and many celebrated actors with their London companies took the stage there. Plays could also be seen at the Theatre Royal in King Street – the oldest theatre in the country, established in 1766 – and the Little Theatre in Colston Street, established in 1923, which was described in Bristol's 1926 Official Guide as one of the leading repertory theatres in the country. Variety entertainment was staged at the Empire in Old Market and the Hippodrome on St Augustine's Parade; both these venues had been established when the popularity of music halls was its height, and for a time maintained their role as places of variety entertainment hosting singers, comedians such as Max Miller and dance companies. By 1920, however, the music hall was under siege from a new competitor: the cinema.

Bristol's first cinema was the Bio, opened in Counterslip Hall in 1908, and by 1920 there were about thirty-five picture houses in the city. Huge crowds flocked to them: their appeal cut across all social classes, although attendance was highest among the least well off for whom the cinema was a place of escape. Cinemas were glamorous. Their architects created palaces; for example, the Bristol architect, William Henry Watkins, designed several including the Regent in Castle Street – one of the largest and finest in the city. Designed in 1926–7, the Regent's interior of red, purple and gold was an opulent fantasy world of florid plasterwork surmounted by an impressive dome. Music was the essential accompaniment to the silent movie. The largest cinemas, such as the Regent, had space for orchestras; soloists were engaged to sing – their repertoire complementing the mood of the film – while many cinemas had organs capable of producing thunderous sound effects. The coming of the 'talkies' came as something of a surprise at first, but they soon ousted the silent film – and the orchestras and soloists. The first showing of a film with sound was Al Jolson's *Singing Fool*, screened at the King's in Old Market. Other cinemas rapidly wired their auditoriums for sound, and by mid-1931 all Bristol's cinemas had been converted. The cinema decimated its competitors. Variety was the chief victim: the Bedminster Hippodrome, opened in 1911, had lasted for only four years as a music hall before being converted to a cinema; the Empire became a cinema in 1931 and the Bristol Hippodrome in 1933.

Twelve new cinemas opened in the 1930s, including the Embassy on Queens Road – Bristol's largest with 2,100 seats – which opened in 1933, and the Odeon, a striking example of modern architecture, opened by Oscar Deutsch in 1938 on the site of the Fry's offices on the corner of Union Street and Nelson Street (see page 64). By 1939 there were some forty cinemas in Bristol distributed widely across the city, from the Savoy in Shirehampton to the Gaiety in Knowle. No other form of entertainment penetrated the suburbs so effectively, and in new areas of housing where amenities were few, cinemas provided a welcome diversion.

Sport occupied many people's leisure time. Some of the large companies such as Imperial Tobacco organised their own football and cricket leagues, and there were many other opportunities for taking part in a wide range of sports including rugby, swimming, golf, cycling, skittles, bowls and billiards. Bristolians could watch association football at Ashton Gate or Eastville, rugby at the Horfield Memorial Ground or county cricket at Horfield. Professional cricket and football attracted large crowds. In 1930, 17,000 people watched Gloucestershire's tie with the Australians in 1930 and in the 1934/5 football season over 47,000 Bristol City supporters (including 5,000 who charged the gates and got in free) saw their team beat Portsmouth 2–0 in a cup fixture. Football pools were a 1930s' creation and widened the appeal of football. They were big business, too: in 1938 £40 million was spent on the pools. Bets were also placed on dogs: greyhound racing took place at Eastville and Knowle stadiums.

There were many other things that people could do for amusement, such as going to the Downs, Bristol Zoo, or the Blaise Castle Estate, which after 1926 was freely open to the public; there was fishing at Blagdon and a choice of trips by motor bus or charabanc to West Country beauty spots such as Cheddar Gorge or Tintern Abbey. In the summer months there were excursions on Campbell's pleasure steamers from the Hotwells landing stage to Ilfracombe, Clevedon, Weston-super-Mare, Lynton or South Wales. There were restaurants, cafes, public houses, museums to visit – or the option of staying at home.

The 1920s and 1930s saw an increase in the importance of home-based leisure activities. Life on suburban estates away from the distractions of city centre life encouraged the development of the home as a centre of private relaxation. Gardening, reading – thrillers and detective stories were all the rage in the 1930s – stamp collecting, knitting and listening to the wireless set were individual forms of relaxation shared by thousands and sustained by commercial interests. The radio spread rapidly from the late 1920s as the mains-powered radio was perfected and householders received electricity: by 1939 nine in ten homes in Britain owned a wireless set. On 3 September 1939 many people in Bristol, as elsewhere, tuned in to their radios to hear the Prime Minister, Neville Chamberlain, announce that a state of war existed between Great Britain and Germany, and over the next six years followed the course of the war by radio news broadcasts.

The war inevitably disrupted leisure and entertainment. The first major raid on Bristol, on the night of 24 November 1940, saw the destruction of the Prince's Theatre and the Regent cinema in Castle Street; five other cinemas went in the blitz and several others were badly damaged. The post-war period saw changes in the pattern of leisure in the city. The remaining theatres survived and flourished: the Bristol Old Vic Company was established in February 1946, and in October that year Sir Laurence Olivier opened the Old Vic Theatre School. The Colston Hall, damaged by fire after the war, was completely refurbished and continued to offer classical concerts and other forms of entertainment, but the cinemas suffered a catastrophic and sudden decline. The attraction of alternative family and home-based activities were the root cause: in particular there was the lure of television which by 1963 was found in 82 per cent of British homes. Increasing car ownership was another factor, extending people's mobility and widening the choice of things to do. And so the cinemas closed to become bingo halls, supermarkets or freezer centres, and by the mid-1960s only a few survived. Just one cinema began showing pictures in this decade – as part of the New Bristol Entertainment Centre opened in Frogmore Street in 1966 – and it started life with a visit from the Lord Mayor and a showing of *Dr Zhivago*.

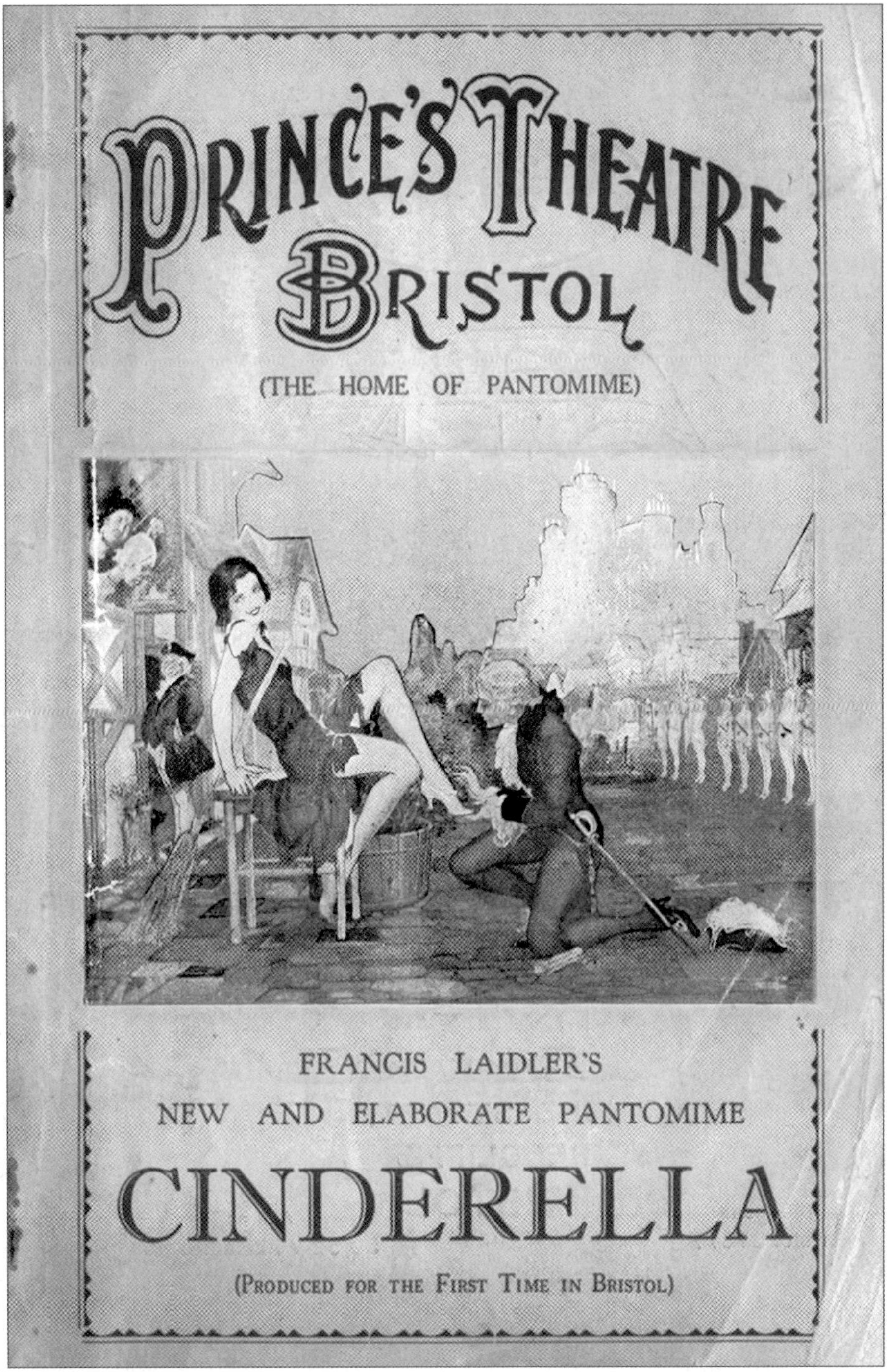

Theatre programme for *Cinderella*, produced by Francis Laidler at the Prince's Theatre, Park Row, commencing 25 December 1937. Pantomine had been a regular feature of the theatre from its opening in 1867. This production starred Phyllis Godden as Prince Charming, Joan Cole as Cinderella with Jack Hayes and Victor King as the Ugly Sisters. The production included dance sequences by the John Tiller Girls and the Turner Twins.

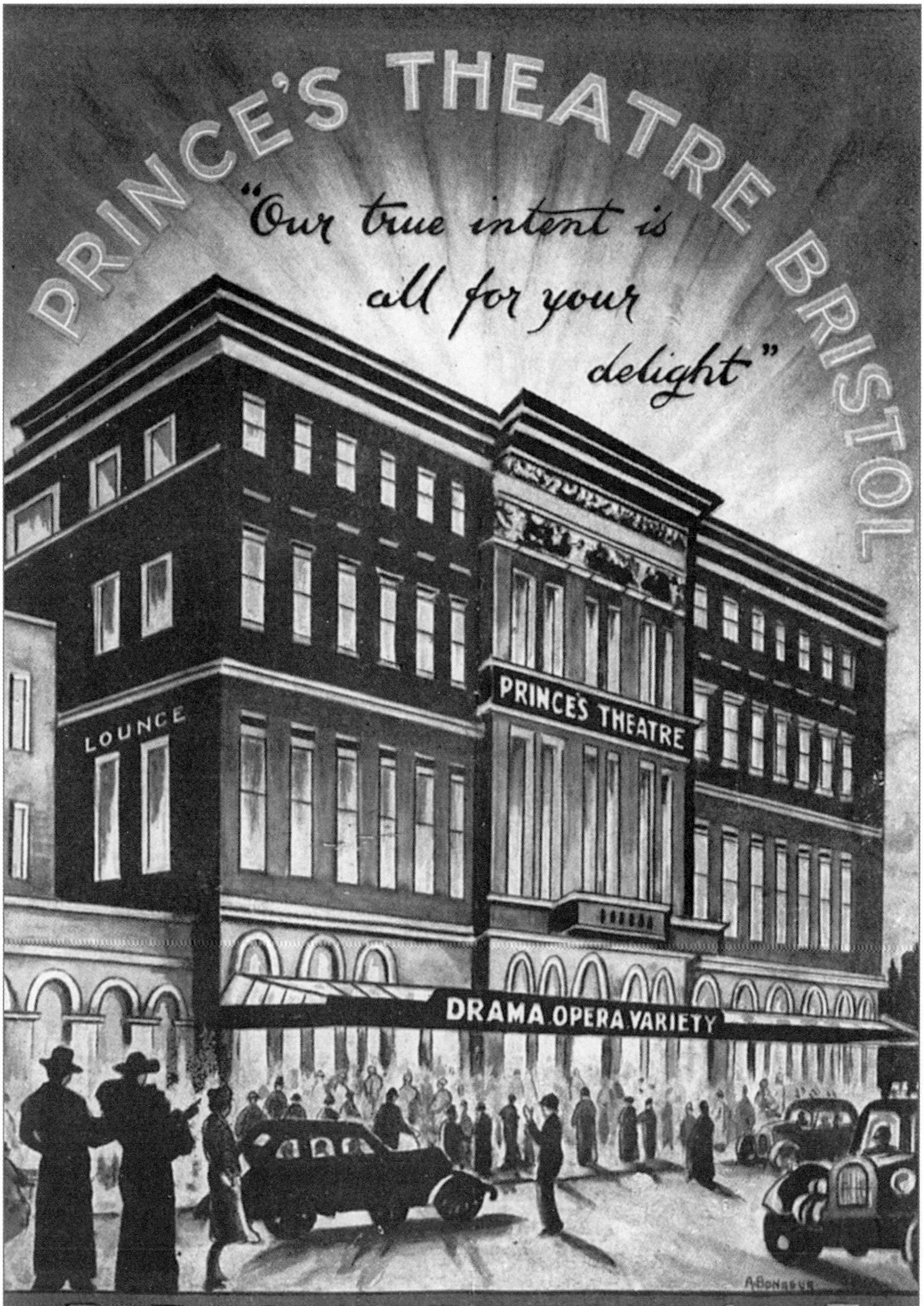

Theatre programme for Verdi's *La Traviata*, performed by the Carl Rosa Opera Company at the Prince's Theatre from 22 April 1940. Seven months later the life of the Theatre Royal came to an abrupt end in the blitz on the night of 24 November 1940.

Amateur dramatics at Bishopston Parish Hall, *The Man in the Bowler Hat*, 20 March 1929. Margaret Sherrell, who is seated second from the left, lived at Downend Park Farm, Horfield.

Queens Picture House, Peter Street, *c.* 1930. This 500-seat cinema was Bristol's first purpose-built cinema and opened in 1910. In 1933 it closed and was replaced by the News Theatre, which had a modern front in glass and chrome; it showed newsreel and cartoon programmes and survived until 1956.

Regent cinema, Castle Street, July 1936. This cinema, with seating for 2,014 people, was built for the Provincial Cinematographic Theatres Ltd and opened in July 1928. It was designed by the Bristol architect W.H. Watkins, who designed several cinemas in Bristol between 1910 and the 1930s. The poster advertises Michael Redgrave with Jean Kent and John Greenwood in the *The Man Within* in Technicolor from Monday 7 July, and also exclusive film of the finalists entering the Rose Queen contest. One of the largest and finest cinemas in Bristol, it had a short life – being a victim of the blitz of 24 November 1940.

The Clifton Suspension Bridge illuminated for the 1951 Festival of Britain. The tradition of illuminating the bridge dates to the opening on 8 December 1864, when arc lights were used.

Ashton Court, 1964. Comprising 850 acres of parkland, Ashton Court was purchased from the Smyth estate in 1959 although the grounds had been open to the public on many occasions for use by the Boy Scouts and the staging of the Bristol Pageant in 1924.

Bristol Zoo, 1950s. Founded in 1835, Bristol Zoo is the fifth oldest in the world. In 1927, after a period of decline, when it was largely used as a fair and venue for fêtes, the zoo developed its zoological and horticultural collections in line with its original objectives. A new aquarium, sea lion pool, new monkey house and polar bear enclosure were built and attendances rose. This view along the Terrace looking towards the aquarium shows the lion house, one of the original buildings, which was replaced in about 1962.

Bristol Zoo, 1950s. The elephant Rosie was a former circus animal acquired by the zoo in 1938; she was very tame and gave rides on her howdah to thousands of children every year. She is seen here in the company of Tom Bartlett, the elephant keeper. Rosie died in 1961.

Entrance to the Blaise Castle Estate, Henbury Road, *c.* 1955. The estate had been in the hands of the Harford family since 1789 but in 1926 they sold it to the City Council which opened it to the public. The walks through the dramatic scenery of the 191 acres of parkland soon made a popular day out for Bristolians. The entrance seen here is just beyond Henbury post office, on the left, which was relocated to Station Road at the end of November 1997. This narrow part of Henbury Road became one way in 1967.

The paddling pool, Blaise Castle Estate, *c.* 1950.

Blaise Castle House, *c.* 1950. Following use of the house by the armed forces during the war, a café was opened, and then in 1949 it became a museum of West of England Folk Life run by the City Council.

Blaise Mansion café, *c.* 1947. This café opened in Blaise Castle House after the war, and was situated in the former picture gallery of the house designed by Charles Cockerell and built in about 1832–3. Run by Civic Catering, the room became a popular venue for wedding receptions in the 1950s and early 1960s. The waitress is Eileen Irwin née Croker, who died aged twenty-seven.

Eastville United Methodist Football Team, 1927. Eastville UM were champions of Wesleyan and Free Church League in 1927.

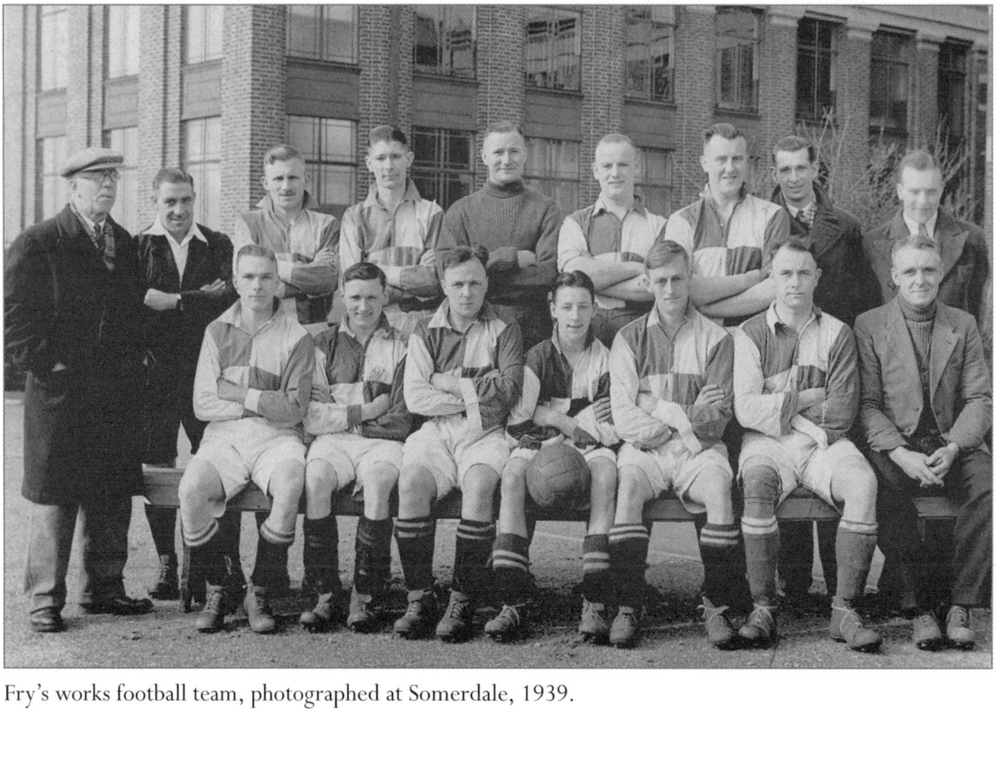

Fry's works football team, photographed at Somerdale, 1939.

CHAPTER SEVEN

LOCAL GOVERNMENT & SERVICES

Local government influence on the running of the city was at its greatest in the mid-twentieth century. From the 1830s, starting with such humble duties as street lighting and establishing a police force, the role of local government widened in the second half of the nineteenth century to include responsibility for public health, parks, cemeteries, libraries and, after 1902, education. The 1919 Housing Act placed the responsibility for housing in the hands of the City, and additional legislation in the 1930s and 1940s further widened the City's authority in the field of health and town planning. The City Council was also a major landowner in Bristol: it managed the largest municipally owned port in the country, and from 1930 was also responsible for the airport.

During this period Bristol was a City and County Borough. In the 1920s the government of Bristol consisted of a Lord Mayor, twenty-three aldermen elected by their fellow-councillors for six years, and sixty-nine councillors representing the various wards of the city elected by the voters of Bristol for three years. The administration of the city was delegated to specialist committees made up of councillors. It was in committees that the important decisions affecting the future of the city were made. There was much prestige and interest, therefore, attached to being a local councillor, although the room for independent initiative was less than it had been in the nineteenth century. The Council was predominantly an instrument of national policy, with roughly 40 per cent of its income derived from government grants. Many of the far-reaching schemes for the building of new council estates and improved health and educational services were born of national legislation: while the Council's role widened in this period, therefore, the initiative lay firmly with central government, and the limitations of the Council's freedom of movement were often only too apparent, as in 1947, when it found its ambitious plans for the rebuilding of the city curtailed by central government; the indignation and dismay of local councillors was considerable but they were powerless.

Most Bristolians saw little of this; the visible side of local government was largely ceremonial. The Council had abolished several ceremonial positions in the late nineteenth century to save money but formal civic occasions were still accompanied by colourful and archaic pageantry. The formal dress of the officials harked back to the eighteenth century, but many of the traditions themselves had their roots in the founding of the Council in 1373. The swearing in of a new Lord Mayor was one such formal occasion when police could be seen holding up traffic at the bottom of Park Street: for a few moments twentieth-century Bristol was held at bay while medieval officialdom – the Lord Mayor, the Sheriff, aldermen and others, led by the City Sword Bearer carrying an eighteenth-century sword – crossed from the Council House to St Mark's, the Lord Mayor's chapel, for a service. The Lord Mayor's chapel is unique in being the only municipally owned church in the country. The opening of the Bristol Assizes was also marked by a formal occasion involving the Lord Mayor, the city's chief magistrate, who joined the visiting judges for a service in the Lord Mayor's chapel. The journey across the centre to the Guildhall where the court was located was an impressive sight: the company travelled in the Lord Mayor's state coach with an escort of mounted police carrying swords; City trumpeters heralded their arrival at the chapel and the Guildhall. This colourful ritual survived until the abolition of the Assize courts in 1971.

The mid-twentieth century saw considerable expansion in the City Council. In 1935 the wards of the city were increased to twenty-three represented by sixty-nine councillors; the following year the number of wards was increased again to twenty-eight and the Council enlarged to 112 members. Following the extension of the vote to women in 1918 and 1928, women entered local politics, and by 1930 there were several women serving on Council committees. Mrs L.M. Pheysey was elected the first woman councillor in 1920 and first woman alderman in 1932; and in 1963 Florence Brown became the first female Lord Mayor. The management and administration of the new areas of responsibility and the expansion of others resulted in a large increase in the City Council workforce. New departments and new posts were established. After 1930 a post of Commandant was created to run the airport, in 1938 the Council appointed its first City Architect and a Planning Department (albeit under the City Engineer) was created in 1947. Before the war the various departments were based in various buildings in the city, while the formal business was conducted in the Council House in Corn Street. By the early twentieth century this was regarded as unworthy of so large and wealthy a community, and in 1919 the Council purchased property on College Green for new municipal buildings. Work was slow to start and it was not until 1935 that the foundation stone was laid, then progress on the building was halted by the war – and it was not opened formally until 1956. Occupying a commanding site on a re-landscaped College Green, the new Council House was the physical manifestation of the central role of twentieth-century local government in the running of the city. By the time of its completion it was not large enough to accommodate the growing workforce, and in 1957 Cabot House was built behind the Council House on Deanery Road for the City Engineer's Department.

The Local Government Act of 1929 brought about major changes in local government. The Board of Guardians established in 1834, which had administered the workhouse system of relief, was abolished and its responsibilities transferred to the Council, which found itself responsible for hospitals, care of the poor and the mentally sick. The Council was now responsible for virtually all the welfare of the city, although charitable and voluntary bodies still continued to support several schools and hospitals with the aid of government grants. There were also several old-established charities in the City responsible for some twenty almshouses which provided several hundred places for elderly persons. Following the 1929 Act Southmead Hospital, formerly administered by the Board of Guardians, was taken over and a Bristol Hospitals Council formed to co-ordinate the work of the voluntary and municipal hospitals in the city. In 1947 the National Health Service was established by the post-war Labour Government to create a completely free and universal health service, and this brought all hospitals under the control of the Ministry of Health. Major hospital extensions in the vicinity of the Bristol Royal Infirmary and on St Michaels Hill – an area which the City Council 'zoned' for hospital use after the war – were built from the late 1950s, including the BRI hospital chimney, one of the city's major landmarks (albeit not a particularly attractive one), which was erected in 1965. The City Council, nevertheless, continued to provide a wide range of health services including the provision of a home nursing service, clinics and health centres, day nurseries and the ambulance service.

The City Council had been responsible for education at both primary and secondary level since 1902, although Bristol was remarkable for the number of its independent schools – some of which were of ancient foundation, such as Queen Elizabeth's Hospital, Bristol Grammar School and Red Maids' School. Developments in local authority-administered schools in the 1920s and 1930s saw a widening of the curriculum, a reduction in class sizes and an improvement in the quality of teachers. In 1919 the City Council's Education Committee established three Bristol Central Schools for east, north and south Bristol. They were intended to fill the gap between the elementary schools and the secondary schools. the latter were subsequently renamed grammar schools and the City provided three of these – Fairfield, Merrywood and St George.The Education Act of 1944 required the City to assess its requirements for education. The rise in the birth rate during the war years, the movement of population to new housing estates and the replacing of the 7,000 school places lost during the war, together with the raising of the school leaving age to fifteen in 1947, resulted in a considerable pressure on school accommodation, and the building of new schools was an important priority for the Council in the immediate post-war years: between 1945 and 1951, fourteen new schools were built. In 1954 the first comprehensive schools were opened at Lockleaze and Hengrove; by 1973 sixty-eight primary schools and twenty-three secondary schools had been built since 1946.

The Bristol Constabulary dates from 1836, and in the second half of the nineteenth century had assumed a wide range of responsibilities including detective investigation, river policing, fire fighting and the provision of an ambulance service. Developments after the First World War took account of changes in society, the introduction of new technology and the huge rise of motor traffic. In 1920 the only motor car in the police force was the Chief Constable's car, but following the passing of the Road Traffic Act in 1930 motor patrols were introduced. The parking of cars in the city centre had become a problem by the 1930s: in 1936, to meet the complaints of motorists of the inadequacy of car parking facilities in the city, the Council issued a pamphlet: 'Where to Park Your Car in the Centre of Bristol'. But the responsibility for policing the arrangements fell to the police, and the problem only worsened in the post-war years as the number of cars increased. In 1961 Bristol was the first city outside London to introduce parking meters, and the same year twenty-five traffic wardens were appointed to ensure that motorists used them – many had threatened not to – and in 1967 they were joined by the first female traffic wardens or 'meter maids'. Police communications improved after 1932 with the introduction of police telephone pillars, which could be used both by the police and the public. They remained a familiar sight in the city until 1968 when personal radios were introduced as part of the unit beat system, where constables patrolled on foot with the backing of a panda car – so called because of their distinctive appearance. The 999 emergency telephone service was another innovation of this period, being introduced in 1946. The Bridewell Street headquarters were rebuilt in 1928 and officially opened in 1930, while new police stations were established at Knowle, Bishopsworth and Lockleaze. Women police first appeared during the First World War and by 1918 there were eighteen on patrol in Bristol. At first they were unpopular with their male counterparts, and were required to patrol in pairs with two men following a few yards behind; and although they formed their own separate division in 1920 it was not until 1931 that women were sworn in as constables.

The City Council provided many other services in the city including libraries, museums, the Colston Hall and the Little Theatre. The care of the streets lay with the Council: the 1930s saw many streets resurfaced with tarmacadam – replacing the granite sets used in the nineteenth century; the City Council also ensured that roads were swept and maintained thousands of street lights. Gas street lamps declined over this period. Electric lamps had first been introduced in 1893 and had been extended to most of the City's principal streets in the Edwardian decade. By about 1930 the use of electric lamps was extended to new roads across the city; gas lighting, meanwhile, remained common in the older nineteenth-century suburbs until the 1950s, but was confined to just a few locations by 1969. The City also emptied the dustbins, carried out food inspections, and its Weights and Measures Department verified and stamped weights and measures and carried out spot checks on the delivery of coal, bread and other articles. The creation of the National Health Service and the nationalisation of the electricity industry by the post-war Labour government removed two important functions from local authority control, but in other fields, such as planning, the role of local government continued to expand, ensuring that the City Council continued to be a major force in shaping the modern city.

The Council House, College Green, *c*. 1960. Over twenty years passed between the laying of the foundation stone of the new Council House, designed by E. Vincent Harris, and its formal opening by Queen Elizabeth II in 1956. This low-angle shot emphasises the long curve of the building and the barren and windswept open space created in front of it when the trees on the Green were cut down between 1950 and 1951. The replica high cross which had stood on the Green since 1850 was also removed.

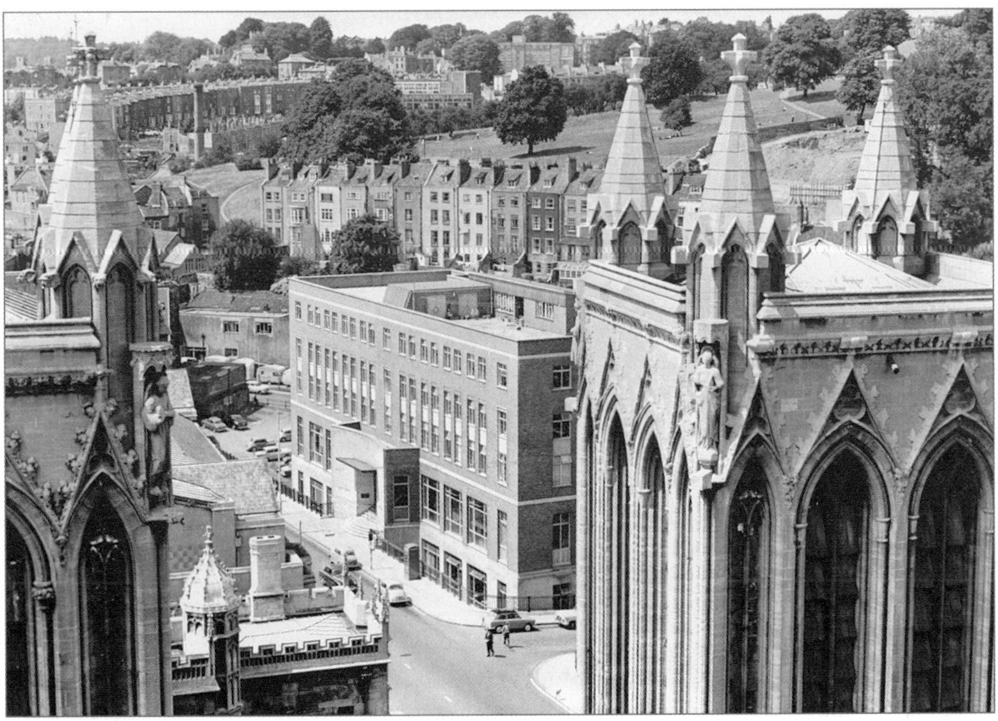

Cabot House, Deanery Road, from the roof of the Cathedral, late 1950s. This block of Council offices was designed by the City Architect, A.H. Clark, and built in 1957.

Red Maids' Founder's Day, November 1959. Red Maids' School was founded in 1634 by John Witson (1557 or 1558–1629), a wealthy Bristol merchant who stipulated in his will that the girls should be clothed in red cloth. The school moved from premises in Denmark Street to Westbury-on-Trym in 1911.

Upper Horfield School, Sheridan Road, Horfield, May 1937. Class 5 is decorated with flags to mark the Coronation of George VI. In this elementary school, which opened in 1929, the children sit behind iron-framed desks with seats and top cut from solid oak.

Ashton Vale Primary School, Avebury Road, Ashton Vale, 8 March 1951. Opened in 1949 to cater for the large number of infants on the new Ashton Vale estate, this primary school was typical of those built after the war by the Education Committee. The informal arrangement of tables and chairs was a far cry from the serried ranks of desks in the older elementary schools. 'All of them', wrote the *Evening World* in 1956, 'are a small world of plastic, plate glass and pastel shades.'

Hengrove Comprehensive School, Petherton Gardens, Hengrove, *c.* 1954. This was one of the first two comprehensive schools in the city, although at first they were called 'mixed' schools to distinguish them from secondary modern and grammar schools. Plans by the Labour group on the Council to expand comprehensive education and phase out the local authority grammar schools evolved around this time and were the subject of much debate.

The Bristol Constabulary Band leads the annual church parade through the city centre to Bristol Cathedral fo
commemorative service in memory of the forty-one officers killed in action in the First World War, *c.* 1936. The ba
which had existed in the 1880s, was revived in 1929 and lasted until the outbreak of war in 1939.

Detectives on church parade, the city centre, *c.* 1936. The detective branch of the police originated in 1880 and beca
the Criminal Investigation Unit in 1920.

Union Street, *c*. 1950. Constable A67 from the Bridewell gives road directions to the driver of a Morris 8 in a desolate post-war city landscape. Relations between the police and motorists have not always been as cordial as this.

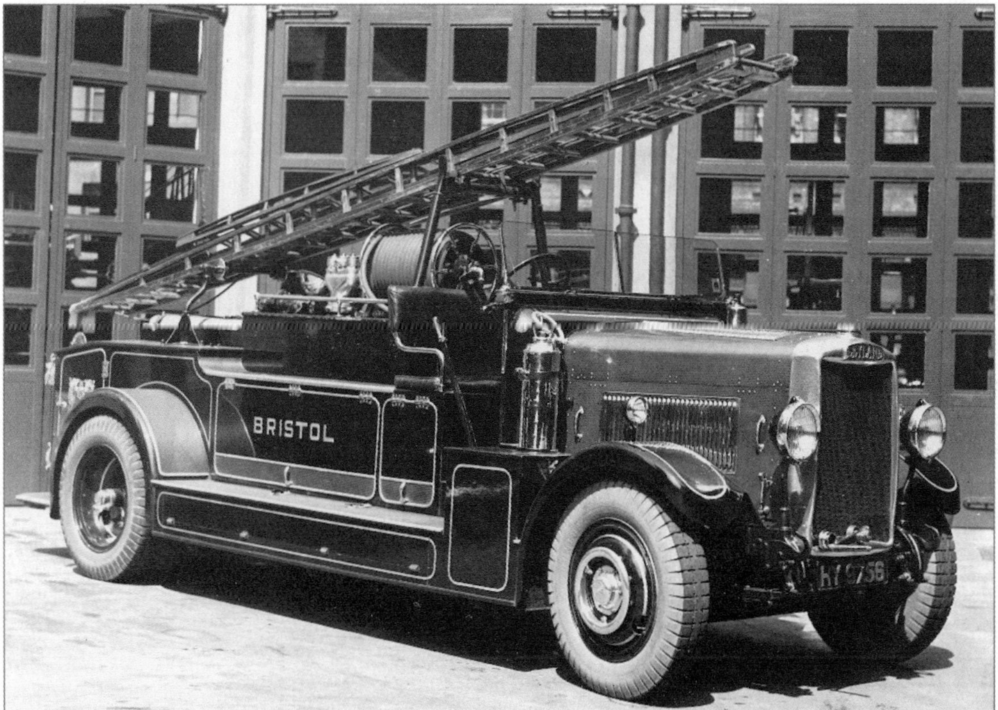

Leyland Braidwood fire engine outside the Bridewell fire station, 1930s. The crew were seated on either side of a box containing the hose and other equipment. This gave no protection from the weather and there was the danger that men could be thrown off when cornering at speed. The new Fire Brigade premises, seen here, were completed in 1930, and in 1935 the strength of the Brigade stood at eighty-five men.

The Central Library, Deanery Road, *c.* 1930. The library was designed by Charles Holden and opened in June 1906. Holden, who went on to design many 1930s London underground stations, adopted a neo-Tudor style for the building. In the 1920s it was the controlling centre for eleven branch libraries in the city and it adopted the open access system in August 1924. The Folk House educational centre, to the right of the library, was bombed in the war. In this pre-war view tramlines are visible in the road.

An extension to the Central Library was proposed as early as 1952 but work did not begin on the building until March 1966; it was opened in July 1967.

Art Gallery, Queens Road, 1950s. The Art Gallery, adjoining the museum, was built by Sir William Henry Wills, later Lord Winterstoke, and was presented by him to the City in 1905; it was designed by Frank W. Wills. In 1928 it was extended by the addition of another wing, also funded by the Wills family. The art nouveau electroliers were made by Thursfield & Co., Birmingham, and the military colours from the Gloucestershire Regiment were presented to the City after the First World War, and remained on display until about 1990.

The Prince of Wales enters the Red Lodge, 6 November 1934. Having spent the morning visiting slum areas and new council housing (see page 113), the Prince of Wales was entertained to lunch by the Lord Mayor at the Red Lodge. This large town house of about 1590 with its well-preserved interior was donated to the City Council by the Bristol Savages, a men-only society of artists, in 1920; public access, however, remained limited until after the war. The Georgian House Museum in Great George Street was opened in 1939.

Bread delivery van, 1940s. A weights and measures inspector checks the weight of a loaf of bread during delivery by a roundsman, using a special balance.

Lulsgate Airport, *c.* 1965. The City Council established an airport committee in 1929 and opened Whitchurch Airport in May 1930; it was then only the third civil airport in the country. Traffic increased steadily after the war and it became clear that Whitchurch could not accommodate the anticipated expansion. Lulsgate Airport, built by the Air Ministry in 1942, was purchased by the Corporation and opened on 1 May 1958. Most of the early services from Lulsgate were operated by Cambrian Airways and Aer Lingus. Two Vickers Viscounts operated by Cambrian Airways on scheduled domestic services are seen in this view.

CHAPTER EIGHT

BRISTOL BLITZED

The Second World War involved the entire nation. For the first time war with another state brought the civilian population into direct contact with the enemy on the Home Front, and people found themselves participating in the defence of their city. Bristol's civil defence involved the creation of volunteer forces of air raid wardens, street fire guards and, in case of a land invasion by the Germans, local platoons of an auxiliary force – at first known as the Local Defence Volunteers; it soon became better known as the Home Guard. Voluntary medical services such as St John's Ambulance Brigade and the British Red Cross Society also played a major role in attending to the wounded. Civilians, therefore, found themselves working alongside the armed forces, the police and full-time fire brigade in the defence of the city. But everyone in Bristol – as in other large cities – was a target as the Germans attempted to destroy civilian morale by night-time bombing of English cities during the bleak winter of 1940/1.

The announcement by the Prime Minister, Neville Chamberlain, on 3 September 1939 that a state of war existed between Britain and Germany at first made little difference to most Bristolians. Street lighting was extinguished and motor cars forbidden to use their headlamps, which led to an increase in road accidents and of people falling into the docks, but there was no immediate German attack. This was the period of the 'Phoney War'. Hitler had been taken unawares by his own success and had made no preparations for the invasion of England. Throughout the ensuing months the strengthening of air defences which had begun in 1937 continued: anti-aircraft guns, searchlights and barrage balloons were deployed around the city. The fear of a gas attack had resulted in the general issue of gas masks in late 1938; they had to be carried at all times and drills on their use were regularly carried out. Surface air-raid shelters were built and Anderson shelters – named after Sir John Anderson, the Home Secretary – were issued free to those with an income below £250 a year. Bristol's civil defence was co-ordinated by the ARP based in Broadmead, and the backbone of the ARP was the wardens' service, which was under the direct control of the Chief Constable.

The first air raid in the Bristol area occurred on 25 June 1940 when the Luftwaffe bombed St Phillips, St Pauls, St James and Brislington although they were actually aiming to destroy the works of the Bristol Aeroplane Company at Filton. There was little major damage although five people lost their lives. Several other relatively minor attacks occurred through the summer of 1940, but a serious attack on the aircraft factories at Filton took place on the morning of 25 September. One Heinkel bomber was brought down by anti-aircraft guns at Portishead – the first of only two enemy aircraft brought down by Bristol's anti-aircraft guns during the war. The other raiders reached Filton and within forty-five seconds had wrought major damage to the plant: ninety-one employees of the Bristol Aeroplane Company were killed and the development of the Bristol Beaufighter, a new fighter plane, was delayed.

With unsustainable losses being suffered during daylight attacks on Britain in mid-October 1940, the Luftwaffe turned to the night bombing of cities, and Bristol suffered its first major raid on 24 November, a Sunday evening. From about 7.00 pm until midnight 134 German aircraft dropped high explosive bombs and incendiaries on Bristol. Fire raged across the city, lighting up the sky and betraying the position of Bristol to enemy air crews from up to 50 miles away. Seventy-seven fire brigades were sent into the city to assist the Bristol force in fighting the fires. The next morning, shattered and dazed, Bristolians walked through the ruins of once-familiar streets filled with the acrid smell of burning, masses of broken glass and the melancholy drip of water. Only a skeleton structure of charred wood remained of the Dutch House; St Peter's Hospital, the jewel in the crown of Bristol's old timber framed buildings, was gone and the Upper Arcade between The Horsefair and St James Barton was destroyed; several medieval churches were badly damaged – St Peter's church, St Nicholas church, St Mary-le-Port church – although their towers all survived; several almshouses were also destroyed. Most of the shops in Wine Street and Castle Street were wiped out and Mary-le-Port Street was totally destroyed; there was also extensive damage in Victoria Street, Redcliff Street and Thomas Street. Clifton also suffered extensive damage: St Andrew's, the parish church, was bombed – although again the tower survived – only to be demolished in 1954. Queens Road, Park Street and Park Row saw extensive damage: the Prince's Theatre was destroyed; so too was the Museum and part of the Art Gallery. There was also damage to the University, including the Great Hall, and Lennards premises on Queens Road was reduced to a pile of rubble. Houses in Bedminster, Knowle and St George were also bombed. The official casualty list included 200 people killed, 163 seriously injured and 526 slightly hurt. The assertion in a German newspaper, however, that Bristol had been wiped out as a major industrial centre was a huge exaggeration, but the scale of the damage revealed how vulnerable the city was to air attack.

The Luftwaffe exploited the inadequacy of Bristol's air defences over the following months, with bad winter weather the city's only effective defence. The next major raid occurred just over a week later, on the night of 2 December, when 167 fires broke out across the city: the Bishop's Palace was destroyed, 156 people were killed and another 149 were seriously injured. The third large air raid took place on the evening of 6 December, and again caused damage to buildings in the centre as well as several industrial sites, including Parnall's aircraft works at Barton Hill. This raid killed 100 people and seriously injured eighty. The New Year began with a large-scale attack by 178 aircraft, which lasted nearly all night. Temple Meads railway station and the City Docks suffered much damage; the Corporation Granary on Princes Wharf was destroyed and St Augustine-the-Less was badly damaged. This was also one of the coldest nights of the year, and fire-fighters and other units had to combat the fires in biting cold and ice. Avonmouth was attacked on 16 January but worsening weather then forced a halt for a while, and the next major raid was not until 16 March. This raid, by 167 aircraft, hit parts of the centre which had previously escaped, and also caused extensive damage in the industrial suburbs of East Bristol; as a result, the casualties were higher on this night than at any time during the war: 257 were killed and 391 were injured. Another raid took place on 9 April and then the last large-scale raid took place on 11 April – the so-called Good Friday raid – when 153 German bombers attacked the city, causing extensive damage in areas close to the City Docks and also resulting in the destruction of Cheltenham Road public library and Colston Girl's School opposite.

The Prime Minister, Winston Churchill, was on his way to Bristol when the Good Friday raid took place, and had to delay his arrival until it was over. As Churchill toured the bomb-scarred city he was booed by some Bristolians who blamed the government for their predicament. Morale was at an all-time low after so much death and destruction during a bitterly cold winter. That Bristol suffered there can be no doubt; the Germans reckoned Bristol was the fourth most bombed city in England. Until September 1941 the enemy killed more civilians than combatants in England, and although morale in Bristol held out – just – many people suffered from considerable stress during the blitz.

From the spring of 1941 the Germans began to turn their attention towards Russia and the heavy raids stopped. There were a few sporadic attacks during the summer of 1941, but they were mainly small-scale affairs. In August 1942 a single bomb from a Junkers 86R flying largely undetected at high altitude fell on Broad Weir, killing forty-five people. The following year passed without a single raid and the final attack by the Luftwaffe on Bristol occurred on 14 May 1944. In over seventy raids on the city 1,250 people were killed, 3,000 were injured and 89,000 properties were destroyed or damaged, but Bristol survived, and industrial production increased through the war years. In May 1945 the people of Bristol celebrated victory and turned to the task of rebuilding the city.

ARP centre, 55 Broadmead, 1940. A rare view of the interior of the Bristol ARP Control, with maps on the wall showing the six ARP divisions into which the city was divided: these were Bedminster, Central, Clifton, Knowle, St George and Shirehampton. The ARP Controller appointed in 1939 was H.M. Webb, the City Engineer.

Gas mask drill in Bristol during the war. The Street Fire Parties, subsequently renamed the Fire Guard, were established to deal with small fires caused by incendiaries; the stirrup pump was their essential piece of equipment. Gas masks were issued in late 1938 and had to be carried at all times; this rule was relaxed by the government after 1942, however.

A dramatic picture of what could have happened if the Germans had released gas on Bristol; this, however, was only a drill.

The Lord Mayor, Alderman T.H.J. Underdown, gives the thumbs up to children being evacuated to Devon in 1941. Over 20,000 children were evacuated from Bristol, chiefly to Devon and Cornwall, from February 1941.

A dawn view of the corner of Broadmead and Union Street, with the Fire Brigade still attending to fires. After the war the building of the new shopping centre started at this end of Broadmead.

The corner of Park Street and Charlotte Street after the air raid of 24 November 1940: a scene of chaos as shocked citizens survey the damage in Park Street. On the night of the raid Park Street was described as an avenue of fire. The telephone kiosk is a K2 concrete model introduced in 1929; it was painted cream and red.

Lennards Corner, Queens Road. This well-known landmark in Queens Road was a victim of the first major raid on Bristol on the night of 24 November 1940. It was described as 'one surging wave of fire' by Eric Buston, a *Western Daily Press* photographer.

Wine Street after the air raid of 24 November 1940. Many fine and historic buildings were lost or damaged beyond repair in the centre of the city during this evening attack, including St Peter's Hospital and the Dutch House – the remains of which were pulled down completely by 6 December 1940. It has been said that the Dutch House proved difficult to demolish: this may have been because of the steelwork inserted when it was refurbished in 1908 (see *Bristol 1850–1919*, page 15), rather than charred seventeenth-century timbers.

Daylight air raid on Broad Weir, 28 August 1942. At 9.30 am a single 500 lb bomb was dropped on the city from a German aircraft flying undetected at over 20,000 ft. It struck Broad Weir near the junction of Philadelphia Street and three buses loaded with passengers were set on fire instantaneously. Many people were trapped in the blazing vehicles and the buses were soon reduced to twisted metal.

Daylight air raid on Broad Weir, 28 August 1942. Forty-five people were killed and twenty-six seriously wounded, while another thirty were slightly hurt; it was the biggest death toll of any single incident.

Unexploded bomb outside 7 Beckington Road, Knowle, 14 April 1943. Dealing with unexploded bombs was an important and dangerous task assigned to the Royal Engineers. This large bomb – Satan – was dropped during the night raid of 3/4 January 1941 and did not explode. It remained buried in Beckington Road for two years until it was recovered from a depth of 29 ft 6 in by Lt Nicholas of the Bomb Disposal Unit, seen on the right. At 8 ft 11 in long without the tail, and weighing 4,000 lb, Satan was the largest bomb dropped on Bristol, and rode in the Victory Parade through London in 1945.

A wartime wedding, 6 March 1943. Jean Brace, a twenty-year-old cigarette packer for W.D. & H.O. Wills, married Ronald Nickless, an RAF pilot, on 6 March 1943 at St Anne's church, Greenbank. The wedding dress was bought with ration coupons from Clark's Bridal Shop in Union Street. Some meat, cakes and tinned fruit were found for the reception before the couple left for three days' honeymoon in Weston-super-Mare.

ARP wardens march past Salmon & Hutchings grocery shop in Shirehampton High Street during victory celebration 1945.

VE Day street party in Shirehampton, 8 May 1945. The war was over and people were able to celebrate at last; pa were held in various parts of the city.

ACKNOWLEDGEMENTS

This book would not have been possible without the kind co-operation of John Williams, the City Archivist, and his staff at the Bristol Record Office who have supplied the majority of the photographs. The photographs on pages 34, 35, 36, 37 and 142 are from Bristol City Museum & Art Gallery and those on pages 55, 88, 93, 94 (top) 128 and 129 are held at the Central Reference Library. Thanks are also due to the Avon & Somerset Constabulary for permission to reproduce the photographs on pages 144 and 145; also to Ivor Aitken for the photograph on page 89; to Mike Hooper for the photographs on pages 103, 132 (top), 134 (top) and 133 (top); and to Denis Williams for the photographs on page 91.

I am indebted to the following for their valuable observations and comments on the text and the photographs: Molly Coghill, Kieran Costello, Paul Elkin, Peter Harris, John Harvey, Mike Hooper, Mike Jenner, Andy King and Karin Walton, and to the staff at Bristol Zoo. I am also grateful to the many people who have given me their time to tell me about life in Bristol between 1920 and 1969. The responsibility for any errors, however, remains my own.

Finally, I would like to thank Simon Fletcher of Sutton Publishing for his enthusiasm and encouragement throughout the project.

BIBLIOGRAPHY

The text of this book has drawn upon a wide range of sources including the spoken record. A wide range of documents was used and some of the most important were building plans, Port of Bristol records, Education Committee records, Minutes of the Housing Committee, Planning Committee documents including the 1952 Development Plan and the 1966 Review, contemporary newspaper accounts, trade catalogues and local directories. The many official guides to the city were useful sources of information, including the Port of Bristol Official Handbooks; most of the local facts and figures quoted in the text are chiefly drawn from such publications. Below is a select bibliography of published works which proved invaluable in the writing of this book.

Anderson, Charles, *A City and its Cinemas*, Redcliffe Press, 1983
Appleby, John B. and other authors, *The People's Carriage 1874–1974*, Bristol Omnibus Company, 1974
Brace, Keith, *Portrait of Bristol*, Robert Hale, 1971
Curtis, M.S., *Bristol, A Century on the Road*, Glasney Press, 1977
Denning, C.F.W., *Old Inns of Bristol*, John Wright & Sons, 1943
Dike, John, *Bristol Blitz Diary*, Redcliffe, 1982
Dresser, Madge, 'People's Housing in Bristol (1870–1939)' in *Bristol's Other History*, Bristol Broadsides, 1983
Elkin, Paul, *Images of Maritime Bristol*, Breedon Books, 1995
English City: The Growth and Future of Bristol, J.S. Fry & Sons, 1945
Hallet, P., *150 Years of Policing in Bristol*, Avon & Somerset Constabulary, 1986
Harrison, David (ed.), *Bristol between the Wars 1919–1939*, Redcliffe Press, 1984
Hasegawa, Junichi, *Replanning the Blitzed City Centre*, OUP, 1992
Lord, J. and Southam, J., *The Floating Harbour*, Redcliffe Press, Bristol, 1983
Penny, J., *The Air Defence of the Bristol Area 1937–44*, Bristol Branch of the Historical Association, 1997
Priest, G. and Cobb, P. (ed.), *The Fight For Bristol*, Bristol Civic Society and Redcliffe, 1980
Priestley, J.B., *English Journey*, Heinemann, 1934
Punter, J.V., *Design Control in Bristol 1940–1990*, Redcliffe, 1990
Ralph, E., *Government of Bristol 1373–1973*, Corporation of Bristol, 1973
Winstone, John, *Bristol As it Was 1963–1975*, Reece Winstone, 1990
——. *Bristol As it Was 1939–1914*, Reece Winstone, 1978
——. *Bristol 1934–1936*, Reece Winstone, 1986
——. *Bristol in the 1940s*, Reece Winstone, 1970
——. *Bristol 1950–1953*, Reece Winstone, 1970
——. *Bristol 1953– 1956*, Reece Winstone, 1969
——. *Bristol As it Was 1956–1959*, Reece Winstone, 1972
Setright, L.J.K., *Bristol Cars and Engines*, Motor Racing Publications, 1974
Shipley, P., *Bristol Siren Nights*, Rankin Brothers, 1943
Somerville, J., *Christopher Thomas Soapmaker of Bristol*, White Tree Books, 1991
Thomas, Ethel, *Down the Mouth: A History of Avonmouth*, Ethel Thomas, 1977 and 1981
Underdown, T.H.J., *Bristol Under Blitz*, Arrowsmith, 1942
Vear, L., *Bedminster Between the Wars*, Redcliffe, 1981
Vincent, M., *Reflections on the Portishead Branch*, Oxford Publishing Co., 1983
Walker, F., *The Bristol Region*, Thomas Nelson & Sons, 1972
Warne, F.G., *The Bombing of Bristol*, Warne, 1943